Richer By India

Richer By India

Myra Scovel

Drawings by Joseph Papin

Harper & Row, Publishers

New York, Evanston, and London

Acknowledgment is made, gratefully, for permission to use material from, or to quote directly, articles which appeared in *Baptist Leader*, January and November, 1961; and in *Concern*, December, 1960.

The author also wishes to thank the editors of *Presbyterian Life* for permission to quote from the article "Destination, India" by Carl G. Karsch, which appeared in the January 15, 1959, issue; and to express her appreciation to Lutterworth Press, London, for permission to quote the passage from Bishop A. J. Appasamy's excellent biography, *Sundar Singh* (1958), page 21.

FIRST EDITION

LIBRARY OF CONGRESS CATALOG CARD NUMBER: 64-13746

For F., always,
and in gratitude to the many Indian friends
who gave this book its title

Because the adventures related in this book
are adventures of the mind,
they take the form that mental adventures always take
—embarking upon quests after meaning,
seeing new shores of thought,
getting shipwrecked and discovering desert islands.

Edmond Taylor,
Richer by Asia

chapter one

"Do you think India will be anything like China?" I asked my husband. He always looks like a Viking when he stands at the rail of a ship.

We had sailed from New York in late April. When we came up on deck that morning of May 16, 1953, the harbor of Bombay was resting upon the water like a jeweled ring on green satin.

"It will probably be very dull after China," Fred replied. "You won't end up in a concentration camp, and you won't have the excitement of an occasional bullet flying through your house."

"I can do very well without excitement," I told him. "After twenty-four years of being married to you, all I want is a good long spell of monotony."

We watched the gulls flash gold as their wings caught the sun.

"But I mean the people," I began again. "You know, will they be like . . . ?"

"Now, remember, we weren't going to compare," he smiled down at me. "We've had to close one door; we're opening another."

"We mustn't forget the N.I.C.s," I added, and we both laughed.

We had been warned that many of the missionaries from China, who had been transferred to other countries, had made themselves slightly unpopular by beginning every other sentence with ,"Now in China, we . . ."

The children had come up on deck and I had been watching them, wondering what they were thinking.

Tom, our blond fourteen-year-old, ping-pong paddle in hand, was watching the land grow larger as we sped toward it. His thoughts were farther away than the horizon.

"I'd better go and pack," said Judy, nervously. She was our brown-eyed eleven-year-old. I wanted to go with her, but knew that she preferred to be alone.

"What time will we get there?" asked nine-year-old Vicki. Her perfectly shaped eyebrows were gathered in a frown from the glare of sun on water.

"Before noon," said her father. "Isn't it exciting? I think I'll try to get a picture."

He seemed to be the only one of us with no apprehensions. Mine dated back to the evening in Stony Point, New York, when he had come home with the news of his impending appointment as Professor of Medicine at the Christian Medical College at Ludhiana in the Punjab, North India.

"Please, not another case of the wanderlust virus," I had said.

But we both knew that this was no mere case of itching feet.

"It will mean uprooting us all again," he said, "and worse than that, it will mean leaving the three older children in America. We can't take Jim and Carl out of college, and Anne ought to finish her nursing course."

I didn't see how I could do it, and only half listened as he told me the reasons why he felt we should go.

"It will sure be good to get back on the mission field where I belong," he continued. "And you know how I feel about the importance of teaching national doctors. I'd be doing just that."

The Christian Medical College at Ludhiana had come to a crisis. The college had been graduating doctors with the licentiate degree in medicine. Now the Indian government had decreed that the college upgrade its curriculum and facilities to give an M.B.B.S. degree—the equivalent of an M.D.

"As they should," said Fred.

The problem was to find staff and provide funds. The government had offered rupees twenty-five laks (about $520,000) toward a new hospital—as a necessary part of upgrading—on condition that the medical college raise the rest of the money needed.

"And money isn't the only problem," Fred went on. "They need qualified staff."

We were sitting before the fireplace in the old Dutch farmhouse provided for missionaries on furlough. Judy and Vicki had gone to bed; Tom was probably doing homework upstairs.

"Have another cup of coffee," I said numbly.

"Thanks. . . . I don't know why they've asked me. Me—a Professor of Medicine! Why, I don't know a thing about medicine!"

"Then how did you get that string of degrees after your name, Doctor Frederick Gilman Scovel?" I asked. "The very reason they've asked you to go to Ludhiana is because they need a man with just your requirements to meet government standards."

"That doesn't mean I can teach," said Fred. "Unfortunately, Mrs. Scovel, the world does not look upon me with love-befuddled eyes, as you do."

"You are a teacher to your finger tips," I said. "You taught doctors and nurses and orderlies and patients' relatives and everyone you could capture with your glittering eye in that blessed old Chinese hospital. That isn't what's worrying me. It's the ——"

"I know," he interrupted. "It's the children. I've thought about them all the way home."

"I simply don't see how I can leave the older three," I said. "And Tom and Judy and Vicki would be torn up by the roots, just as they're making new friends here."

"We don't have to make any decision tonight," Fred reminded me, setting down his coffee cup and reaching for my hand. "We'll take plenty of time to pray about it. If this thing is right, it is right all the way."

The next morning I looked around the kitchen as I set the table for breakfast. If I were to say yes to Fred's proposition, it would mean giving up all this. It would mean going back to a kitchen tracked with charcoal from bin to stove; checking to see that the cook's hands were clean, that the dish towels and aprons were clean—and they never would be what I would call clean. It would mean seeing that all our drinking water was boiled, that the salads were safe for us to eat. It would mean never getting my hands in the warm suds of a family wash, never smoothing the frill of a dress with an iron, never hanging clothes on a line in the sun.

In short, it would mean coming down off my throne as a homemaker, and yielding that throne to someone I would have to see do a poor job of it. Visas were not granted by the government to anyone who could be replaced by an Indian in that job, and I knew that the Indian government and I would never agree on who could best keep my house.

Actually, I knew that Fred's visa would not be refused because his wife wanted to do her own housework. But the principle of the government's visa-granting remained. I had gone through all this thinking before. I knew that there were better ways for me to help than by keeping some deserving cook from getting the job he needed to keep his family alive.

It was still early, and I walked out to see if the lilacs in the

4

side yard were in bud. Perhaps under the sky, I could think more clearly. I realized that if Fred turned down this job, he might never again be able to look himself in the face. From the time he was nine years old, he had known that he was going to be a medical missionary. He believed in the overseas mission of the Church, and he knew that one way he could carry out that mission was to train national doctors to meet the overwhelming needs of the sick in their own countries. Specialists in internal medicine did not grow on trees. If he turned his back on this call of Christ to go and heal, he would slowly die inside.

"We'd be right there on the front line," he had said. "After seeing China go to the Communists when we thought it could never happen—well, you never know how much more time there is. Since the Indian Church has asked me to come, I'd like to be doing what little I can to train Indian doctors to carry on."

The Communists. Yes, I had to face it—I was afraid. I had looked forward so much to our staying in America after twenty-one years on the mission field in China. Six of those years we had been virtual prisoners of the Japanese, and we had spent six months in a concentration camp. We had been repatriated on the last trip the Swedish liner *Gripsholm* made from the Orient. If Vicki had not been three weeks overdue, she would have been born at sea, and we would have had a Swede in the family. "GRIPSHOLM" RACES WITH STORK had made headlines.

Not content with all this, our family had gone back to China. We hadn't been there long before the Communists took over. We moved south ahead of them—Fred teaching medicine and I working as a nurse. After Canton fell, we had a year and a half of neat poison under the Communist regime. But we were among the fortunate, and had been allowed to leave.

"Allowed to leave" is a strange way of putting it. We had escaped we knew not what, though we had seen enough to make a clear guess. But how we hated being forced out of the country we loved so deeply—to be torn from our Chinese friends! It was difficult to think of spending the rest of our lives away from them—never again to speak with them in the language in which together we had laughed and suffered. China had been home to us for most of our married life; our children had been born or brought up there, and there God had been very close to us. Our sense of infinite relief at being free was colored by sorrow, fear for those friends, a heavy heart.

But oh, we were grateful for our freedom. To be alive in a land where there was recourse to justice, where truth was respected and sought, made one believe in all miracles. I did not want to jeopardize our precious freedom another time. I did not ever want to go any place again. I wanted to build a house in Stony Point—just once to unpack everything we owned, to set Grandmother's Chinese cabinet against a wall and never, never move. . . .

"Mother, where are you?" called Judy from the porch.

I had been outside longer than I had intended; the children were already in the kitchen. Tom was making toast for himself and the girls.

"What has four legs, a flat top, and bristles?" asked Judy as she poured the orange juice.

"I'll bite, Judy. What does have four legs, a flat top, and bristles?" asked Tom, always ready to step into the breach as straight man.

"A chair, a table, and a toothbrush," Judy replied.

"We'll treat that with the silence it so richly deserves," said Tom.

"I don't see anything funny about it," said Vicki, sleepily. She was never fully awake until she got out to the bus stop corner with her schoolmates.

"Children, how would you like to go to India?" asked their father, coming into the kitchen.

6

If I had subconsciously hoped for a violent reaction against such a query, I was disappointed.

"When do we start?" asked Tom.

"Can I take my doll and carriage?" asked Vicki.

"And all our dolls, and all our things, and not leave anything behind?" added Judy.

"Now, nothing is settled at all," I put in, "but pray about it when you say your prayers. We want to do only what God wants us to do."

"Do I really believe that?" I asked myself after the last school bus had gone. The question stayed with me as I did the housework. By the time Fred got home that night I was ready with my answer. None of my problems had been solved but there was a certain peace in knowing that God would go with us every step of the way.

I waited to tell Fred when we were alone. His face had the look of a boy on Christmas morning when I said, "I'll go to India with you. I'd follow you to the ends of the earth—mostly because I wouldn't trust you out of my sight. But I warn you; the first time I see a snake, I'll turn around and go home."

He didn't take that last bit at all seriously. "It's late. Let's get to bed," was all he said.

I wasn't fooling about the snakes. I was psychopathic in my fear of them. I had been told too many skin-prickling stories like the one of the woman who was locked in a room with a dead cobra. Her husband thought that she would thus see how harmless it was, and get over her fear of snakes. The story has no such happy ending. The cobra's mate, bent on revenge, crawled in through a chink in the floorboards and killed the woman. There were other stories equally cheering. I would break out in a cold sweat at the thought of a cobra's head dilating before me.

And here we were at the Gateway to India, and the thought of snakes never entered my mind.

7

chapter two

We were in high excitement by the time the ship maneuvered its way into port. We could hardly wait to be done with the formalities and get out into the streets. Fortunately, Harold Ruch was on hand to see us through. He was an old China friend, now our Presbyterian mission representative at the Inter-Mission Business Office.

As we came from the customs shed into the sunlight, the first thing that struck us was color. Here in Bombay, the sun was not just sunshine; it was yellow gold spilling over the streets, casting deep purple and blue shadows into the corners which it could not fill. The men's clothing was so much whiter than white. And the saris! Such reds, such turquoise, such greens and blues!

There were no jerky movements. The women glided along the streets in their flat, thonged sandals; the men moved at a slow, even pace. The children were content to cling to the hands of their elders and become a part of the flow of color and rhythm.

9

As we walked along looking for a taxi, we were amazed to find that there were so many different kinds of Indians. There were tall, turbaned, bearded Sikhs (we had known them in Shanghai as efficient traffic policemen); there were men and women with very light-cream complexions—"Kashmiris," Harold told us; and there were those who were as dark-skinned as some of the Africans walking by. There were people from every country in the world, it seemed. We tried to guess from which country each one came; Harold would set us right if we missed.

"Let's stand still for a minute and listen," said Judy.

For all the noise, there was a quiet, a hush, in Bombay—as if it were poised, listening for something. Being Americans, we had no time to wait to hear what that something might be. We had to leave at once for Landour where Fred and I would study Hindustani, and where Tom, Judy, and Vicki were to attend Woodstock School.

Harold managed to get reservations for us on the night train for Dehra Dun. And, since he had a previous engagement, arranged to have a fellow missionary, the Rev. Harry Shaw, take us to the railway station. The trip would take us northward across India to the foothills of the Himalaya Mountains.

At the station platform, Mr. Shaw skillfully guided us along a path strewn with straw baskets of vegetables, crates piled higher than our heads, food stalls on wheels, and people, people, people. We were to be in a second-class compartment. It turned out to be a large, wooden box of a room, with six hard leather-covered berths. After the crowded third-class coaches we had passed on the platform, it seemed luxurious, if dirty.

"We must be in the wrong one," I said, as Mr. Shaw motioned the porters to set down the luggage. "There are two men in this compartment."

"Oh, don't worry about that," said Harry Shaw. "There may be more than two before morning."

Ummmm! How did one manage about sleeping! One just spread out a bedding roll and slept. Slept? The incessant humming of three small fans made it seem even hotter than it was—until the fans went off for an hour; then the heat was like a blast from a steel furnace. And it was dirty—gritty, sooty, sweaty dirty. Judy's and Vicki's faces were smudged with black. Miraculously, Tom still looked clean. Judging from the occasional snorts in the berth above me, Fred was already sound asleep. I was so placed that I could not see our Indian companions.

My mind kept going back to our three children whom we had had to leave in America. Nothing would ever make this long separation from Jim, Carl, and Anne seem right. The cost of that decision was the one sacrifice I made in being a missionary.

If only I could throw off this blanket of heat! I decided to think of the coolest, cleanest, loveliest place that I could remember. Lan Tau, the hill island rising from the sea near Hong Kong— that was it. I could hear the swish of the long grass in the wind; I could see the wild orchids. . . .

I was jolted awake as dawn was breaking. We were slowing down for a station. All three of the children were peering over their berths, their eyes fixed in the direction of our traveling companions. I twisted myself around to see what was happening. The man in the upper berth was still asleep, but the man in the lower, a swarthy Sikh, was combing his hair—very long, black hair, which he wound in a knot on the top of his head, then tied with a handkerchief to hold it there. I, too, watched fascinated, as he wound the six yards of beautiful red-pink silk into a smooth, pleated turban. He then went to work on his beard, twisting it deftly, and securing the longer bits behind his ears.

"These men are Sikhs," I thought. "Here is where I should begin my missionary work. I should get up and engage them in conversation."

Perhaps because I was lethargic from the heat, or lazy, I continued to lie on my hard bunk. I told myself it was because the children were taking turns washing in the dirty little toilet room.

In the meantime, Fred had jumped lithely down from his upper berth, and simply because he was interested to know, discovered that one of the travelers was a medico-legal man, the other a dealer in manganese. The conversation continued through the breakfast the men helped us to buy at a station.

"And what are you doing in India?" asked the one with the Oxford accent.

Fred told them simply why he had come to India and what he hoped to do here. He had had a golden opportunity, and he had not let it pass, though I knew that he had never once thought of it as "an opportunity." He liked people. It was natural for him to want talk to them.

Our Sikhs said goodbye to us at Delhi.

We spent another hot night on the train. Morning found us awake, laughing at our stiff wire hair. Faces washed, hard-boiled eggs eaten, we were ready, now that it was cooler, to enjoy the last lap of our journey.

"Look! Monkeys!" cried Vicki.

"Oh, hello, Vicki," said Tom, waving to one of them.

I cut that one short, and we watched the monkeys loop from tree to tree. The train crawled up through the pass in the hills, crossed the plateau, and pulled up at the station in Dehra Dun.

"I rather dread meeting Doctor Strickler after his tragedy," Fred whispered to me as he hauled out the suitcases.

We had read about it in American newspapers while we were packing for India, and had had to remind ourselves that the same thing could as well have happened in our own New York State.

Tall, kindly Herbert Strickler waved to us from down the platform. As he hurried toward us, we saw the lines of suffering on his face, but he greeted us warmly, trying not to burden us with his sorrow. .

13

We drove to a compound of grass, shrubs, and flowerbeds—to a spacious house kept cool and dark by overhanging trees. The servants had prepared a delicious lunch, but the house was empty of the one who had made it a home. After the children were in bed that night, our host told us what had happened.

He had been away on a trip for the mission. His wife was alone except for a visitor—a new teacher who had just come to Woodstock School. That night, their house had been entered by two young men looking for hunting guns or money, or both. Entering through the guest room, the men were surprised to find a visitor in the house. They had tussled with her and killed her with knives. Mrs. Strickler, hearing the cries, had run at once to the guest room where the thieves attacked and killed her, too. The men escaped with a few trinkets and a watch, through whose serial number they were later traced and convicted.

"If only I hadn't left her!" said Herbert Strickler. He covered his face with his hands for a moment, then straightened, "But I had to go to that meeting. There were problems . . . Martha had often stayed alone before. Martha was never afraid to be alone."

The house was quiet as his voice dropped. Much too quiet.

"Come, I must show you the lights on the hills above us," he changed the subject. Going over to the long French windows, he pulled aside the drapes and beckoned us to see the lights on the mountain—the hill station, Landour.

"There's where you'll be getting a start on your Hindustani," he said. "Don't stint on your language study. There is nothing more important than knowing the language well."

We would be living up there in those Himalayan foothills. Our children would be going to school each day. Life would go on for us normally and happily—unless some blow should strike, as it had struck this man now living alone in his grief, bravely carrying on the work he had come to India to do.

With a sigh, he let the heavy curtain drop from his hand. I wanted very much to leave on the next train for Bombay. I wanted very much to go home.

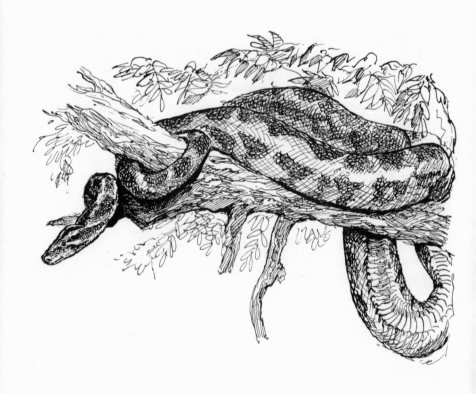

chapter three

We had been in Landour three weeks when I saw my first snake. Fred and I were walking along a narrow trail on our way home from the morning session of language school. We had been looking down at the plain below through the dry haze of dust that lay over everything. It would be another month before the monsoon rains broke. We could hardly make out the city of Dehra Dun below. It looked hot down there—very hot.

"My, but it's good to be out of that heat," said Fred. "Harry Shaw was certainly right. May or June is no time to travel in India. Look OUT!" The last was a shout.

A long snake—we differ as to its exact length—was slithering down the hill toward us. It lightninged across the path just missing my feet, and disappeared into the bushes below.

Fred will take oath that I rose three feet in the air, took three steps and then came down.

"The poor little thing," he said. "You've frightened it."

"Oh, I have, have I?" I said when my heart stopped pounding enough for me to get my breath. "The 'poor little thing' hasn't

17

done a thing for my equilibrium. You can take your dear little snake and jump over the next cliff."

"You don't mean that," he said, catching up with me and kissing the top of my head. "Who would protect you from these huge, dangerous pythons if *I* didn't?"

I was still shaking when I got to the house, either from fear or from wrath at his nonchalance—perhaps both.

But I could never remain cross at him long, and secretly I was a bit pleased, for I had taken my first encounter better than I had expected.

We had a good lunch of our favorite peanut soup and lettuce sandwiches. (The children took their lunches to school.) When we had finished, the cook came in to take the daily accounts, and to hear what I planned for the next day.

Chandru, the cook, was a man with the brow of a philosopher, the large round eyes of a child, and the soft musical voice of all hill people. On the way to India I had prayed that God would guide us to the servants he wanted us to have. When our neighbor, Virginia Parker, first introduced us to Chandru, I felt that I already knew him. She was from our Western India Mission and was leaving Landour after her son's graduation from Woodstock. We were fortunate to be getting her cook and to be moving into the house which she was vacating.

How Chandru prepared such delicious meals in his dark corridor of a kitchen, I do not know. Even more of an enigma was how he managed to find what he wanted to use from the assortment on his shelves: dishes, shopping bags, pots and pans, meatboard, cleaver, paper bags filled with spices, his clean socks, knives, spoons, garlic, wilted stalks of green onions, his "white" coat for serving at table, apricots, and what I thought at first were dust cloths, but turned out to be dish towels.

His young nephew was apprenticed to him—a shy, curly-haired boy called variously Bahadur (his real name), Balu (Little Bear), which we called him, and Joe.

Chandru never seemed to mind having the children crowd into the kitchen with him and his nephew. We should have paid him double for his language lessons to our three. He had a quick perception, and with few words the children were able to communicate with him. Tom discussed mountain climbing; Judy had her first lessons in Indian cooking. One day I heard Vicki tell him in broken Hindustani, "The cat's baby isn't. I don't know whether it has gone up [pointing to heaven] or down." With almost no English, Chandru assured her that there is an afterlife for kittens, and that this one had surely gone to heaven.

If only Fred and I could have found such a short cut to learning this difficult language! The grammar alone made Latin look like a Dick and Jane reader.

"Taj, you're going to have to help me," Fred said to his private teacher one day. Mr. and Mrs. Taj, the Indian couple who taught us, were arriving for our afternoon session at home. "I know four different ways to say 'God' in this language," Fred went on, "but I can't even ask a man if he has a pain, and if so, where."

"I know, I know," replied Taj, who seemed to have only one name. Settling his portly frame in a large wicker chair, he continued, "Tell me some of the questions you will want to ask your patients, and their probable answers, and we'll write out some sentence cards for you to study."

"You see, this beginners' course was designed to introduce Hindustani to missionaries, most of whom are ministers." Daisy defended her institution in her deep, husky voice. We were seated at opposite ends of the glassed-in porch which was our living room.

The Tajs had been assigned to go down to the plains with us to teach us in Ludhiana; but first we had to complete the language school's summer course at Landour. After twenty-one years of speaking Chinese, this was not an easy task for the language school—nor for us!

Fred and I climbed the steep hill to Kellogg Church each morning. Here we met in small classes of five to ten students each, in different parts of the community church building which was the language school's summer headquarters. We would sit there, holding the heavy green grammars in our laps, comparing the diagrams of throat and mouth with the way our teachers made the sounds. How could we manage to pronounce "d" in four different ways?

The hours we spent in those red-cushioned pews should have made us fluent in several languages, but we could seldom remember the past pluperfect verb-ending, and the sentence would hang there, suspended in the stale air of the church. (I learned later that since verbs end the sentence in Hindustani, verb endings are really of very little use; you have only to pause before you reach them, and the quick-witted Indians will end all sentences for you.)

Here at the school, we also had several sessions a day with different private tutors. One of our teachers had strong Communist leanings, with convictions of what he "knew" to be true about Communism. After our year and a half of living under Communism in China, his "truths" were not always easy for me to take, though Fred remained very philosophical about them.

"But this is just where we came in, in China," I wanted to blurt out. Our teacher had an explanation for every fact we told him of our firsthand experiences—explanations which satisfied him completely, and left me smoldering inside. So many of his sentences were, word for word, the same sentences we had heard in China.

"Doesn't your hard-won freedom mean anything to you?" I asked one day, trying not to let my exasperation show through. "An individual has no freedom under a Communist regime. We've lived under it; we know."

"Ah, yes, Mrs. Scovel, but you see you are a foreigner. Excuse me, but this is true. It is . . . well, natural that your freedom would be curtailed, but the Chinese people are no longer under the oppression of rich landowners. Besides, the individual is not important in comparison to the glory of the state."

"The glory of the state." "No longer under the oppression of . . ." How many times had we heard it all? It was useless to speak of the lack of personal freedom, of the hunger, of the fear, of the disruption of families. Would India, then, have to learn the hard way? I did not want to be here when she did. This teacher was young enough to be my son. His beautiful teeth would gleam as he smiled at me indulgently. I wanted very much to shake some sense into that youth. It was three years before I realized that, left to herself, India would never choose Communism.

The language study itself was not so frustrating to me as it was to Fred. Hindustani is a mixture of Urdu, used to the north of Ludhiana, and Hindi, used to the south and the national language. To me, studying it was like opening a surprise birthday package. It was exciting to find the words which had come to us from India—to discover that *cummerbund* meant "to bind the loins"; that *kakhi* meant "dust"; that *pajama* meant "pajama" and always had; that *mistri* was a transliteration of the English word "mystery" and meant "craftsman," just as the English word had originally.

Fred had no time to indulge in derivations. He had to know how to communicate with his patients. This meant that he had to complete the regular course, and learn all he could of the medical vocabulary from his private teachers. He did not like language study in the least, and was impatient to get to his work in Ludhiana. There were those who argued that he would not need the language, that he could use an interpreter. Fred could not conceive of an interpreter standing between him and those he was attempting to heal.

"How can you treat a man's illness if you can't get the feel of all that lies behind that illness?" he would ask.

"You are completely right," Taj would reply. One day he added, "You two have been working very hard. It's time you had an Indian meal cooked by Daisy."

This was our introduction to Indian food, and we were invited to many more wonderful meals cooked by Daisy. Here we got our first taste of *pukka* curry, saffron rice, mango chutney, and many other delectables. (That ubiquitous word, *pukka*! It seemed to become a part of the vocabulary of every foreigner with any connection to India. It meant "tops," "ripe," "traditional," "in-the-groove," a "brick house" rather than a mud-brick one, "according

22

to the accepted pattern," a "gentleman," "cooked," "reliable," and many, many more things. Daisy and Taj, who were excellent teachers, tried in vain to explain it; we had to pick up for ourselves when to use it, and we soon did.)

The Tajs lived at the top of a hill, with a view of the great Himalayas beyond. At least, they assured us that the mountains were there, and promised us that the dust haze concealing them would be washed away completely by the monsoon when it came.

Tom, Judy, and Vicki liked Indian food at once; we all did. The peppery hot things did not trouble us too much.

"But I was sparing of the spices," said Daisy, laughing happily, her smooth black hair catching the light of the fire as she came in from the kitchen.

After dinner, we persuaded Taj to tell us about his father and Praying Hyde—a story he had hinted at during our study sessions. Taj loved to tell a story, and could do so like a professional. When he spoke, his deep, rich voice rolled all the consonants, and savored the vowels. Tom edged his chair nearer to this artist as he began.

chapter four

"Praying Hyde was a remarkable man," said Taj. "He gathered around him a few promising young men who were greatly attracted to his way of life—his voluntary poverty, his identification with village poeple. They called themselves 'The School of the Prophets,' and my father was one of them."

But the Rev. John Hyde, a Presbyterian missionary known far and wide as "Praying Hyde", had been, apparently, somewhat of a trial to the other missionaries of his day. He gave everything he owned to the poor—and when his overcoat and bedding were gone, he would give away the blanket on the next bed, never dreaming that the lady of the house might object.

"One day his Indian evangelist rebuked him for giving his last blanket to a worthless boy," said Taj. " 'Ah, friend, friend,' Hyde replied, 'if the Prodigal Son had come home to you, you would have taken a stick to him.' "

Hyde never spared himself. Once while he was on a preaching tour of the villages, he was taken with an excruciating headache. He urged his disciples to go on with their plans for the day, and asked them to move his bed out under the trees before they left. The women of the village, curious to see this strange man, gathered around him. Sick as he was, he talked with them.

"Evangelistic work among women had been at a standstill in that village," said Taj. "Yet that evening, after Hyde had spoken to them and prayed with them, they all asked for baptism."

"Another thing about him," Taj went on, "was that he never for a moment doubted that God would answer prayer. When we lived in Moga, my father often pointed out to me the field where Hyde had paced back and forth, praying for a house. He was living and working in Moga at the time, and wanted to start a school. The Hindu political group, the Arya Samaj, were worried that the Christians were increasing, and they got everyone to refuse to sell land or buildings to Hyde."

Taj turned to Fred. "You've probably heard of the famous eye specialist who lived in Moga, Dr. Matthura Das. He was planning to move his eye hospital into the city. Though he was a Hindu, he said he would sell Hyde the house he was then using, so Hyde could have it for his school.

"But Hyde had no money with which to purchase it. That day, he took my father and his other disciples into the field for prayer. They asked that God would provide them with the needed money. Suddenly Hyde shouted in Hindustani, '*Bol! Yisu Masih ki Jai!* Proclaim! Victory through Jesus Christ!' He told his friends that they needn't ask anymore; that they should now give thanks to God for having answered their prayers. My father was puzzled, but he believed his teacher knew whereof he spoke.

"When Hyde got to the street corner, he went up the steps of the Queen Victoria statue and shouted again, 'Proclaim! Victory through Jesus Christ!' "

Now Taj's voice dropped to almost a whisper. "That very day, Hyde Sahib went to Jagraon. Miss Jenks, one of the missionaries, said that she had two thousand rupees, a tithe from a friend in America, and that she had been led by God to give him that money. The other three lady missionaries joined Miss Jenks, and the four gave three hundred rupees each from their own money. Hyde went on to Ludhiana where he found a check awaiting him from an anonymous donor. This exactly made up the amount he needed for his school."

Taj could not vouch for the accuracy of the story that at one time the senior missionaries, exasperated beyond endurance at Hyde's failure to write reports and keep his records up-to-date, or to remember when he had a committee meeting, requested the Board of Foreign Missions in New York to recall John Hyde. They said he did very little work and spent most of his time in prayer. The Board is said to have cabled back: LET HIM PRAY.

One story Taj *could* vouch for was of the very first time his father had ever preached. "Praying Hyde was to have conducted the service himself," Taj said, leaning forward in his chair with an air of mystery. "Instead, he turned the whole service over to my father. 'You can do it,' he told his young disciple. 'I will go outside and pray for you.'

"My father had no time to prepare a sermon. He went to the pulpit and announced a hymn. After the hymn he prayed, and the prayer seemed to flow from his lips.

"Now it was time for the sermon," Taj said dramatically. "As my father stood in front of the congregation, he looked up, and there before his eyes, a scroll unrolled itself in mid-air. On it was written a text. Dumfounded, my father read it. Then sentence by sentence, the whole sermon appeared on the scroll. All my father had to do was to read it off. And the congregation said they had never before heard such a moving sermon."

"I will tell you something that may comfort you," Taj went on.

27

"Hyde had great difficulty with the language. At one time he was in such despair over mastering it that he sent in his resignation. A letter from the village people of his area followed immediately, begging that Hyde's resignation not be accepted. 'If he never speaks the language of our lips, he speaks the language of our hearts,' it read."

(Blessed, perceptive people, who could see beyond words to meaning!)

"Hyde lived in the very house in Ludhiana where you are going to live," said Taj.

"In *our* house?" gasped Judy and Vicki in one breath.

"Yes, and judging from the floor plan your mother showed me, when you two are home from boarding school you will be sleeping in the very room where he slept," Taj replied.

"Wow! That scares me," said Judy with a shudder.

"Oh, no, you musn't be scared," said Taj. "Hyde was a very happy person and liked a joke as well as your father does. One day a rather worldly woman, who thought she would have fun at Hyde's expense, said to him, 'Mr. Hyde, do you think that a lady who dances can go to heaven?' Hyde replied, 'I do not see how a lady could go to heaven and not dance!'

"When we get to Ludhiana, I'll see that you meet old Padri Samuel Baldeo," Taj said, as he turned to Fred. "He is ninety-one years old—reads without his glasses—urges everyone who comes near his bedside to accept Christ as Savior. He knew Hyde well. Padri Baldeo told me once that when Hyde went to visit the sick and found the children dirty, he himself would help wash the children's hands and feet. How he won over the parents of those poor children!"

"I wonder if a man like John Hyde would ever get to the mission field today," said Fred. "All these psychological tests—all this talk of adjustment . . ."

"Hyde simply could not conform," said Taj. "It could be very exasperating to those who were carrying out a program. He would board a train for the all-important annual meeting, but on the way he was sure to meet a Punjabi villager who needed him. Hyde would go on home with the man, and never get off at the station where the meeting was to be held."

I hated to suggest that it was time to leave, but the hour was late, and there was school for all of us in the morning.

Since Daisy and Taj were to go with us to Ludhiana to continue teaching us there, it looked as if language study on the plains would have some fascinating moments. Now, Fred was not the only one who was anxious to get to Ludhiana.

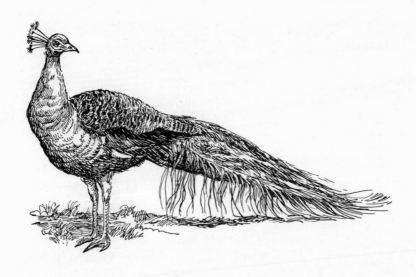

chapter five

But leaving Landour for Ludhiana would mean another separation from our children. This time we would not have one of the six with us. We would have to leave the younger ones in those dormitories I could see below me, perched precariously on the ridge. (In Landour, one had to climb up or down even to empty the garbage at one's back door.) The children would have to hike several hundred feet straight up from their dormitories to the school. Climbing would be even more dangerous after the monsoon rains came and the soil was loosened. Fred assured me with an expression he often used when I worried. "Calm down; more people die in bathtubs than are kicked to death by mules."

There was no danger of our drowning in bathtubs; there was not enough water for that. Everything we saw, touched, or smelled was chalk dry. The hills below us were streaked with chalk; our shoes scuffed up chalk dust. Our hair was dry, our skin was dry, the air we breathed was dry. As our water supply got lower, and the taps gave only a dry cough for more and more hours each day, I had moments of quiet panic. What if the rains didn't come? I managed to make a joke of it to Ernestine Sauer, a neighbor.

"The monsoon rains always come," she said as she poured my usual cup of coffee.

I went back to my dusting three times a day, and tried to believe that the rains might come even this year. The clouds would form, and I would hope. But not one drop of rain fell.

Then, one evening at dusk, when I was alone in the house, there was a sudden loud crack of a giant whip, and lightning cut the sky a jagged scar. I ran to the front door as the first drops of rain began to sound on the tin roof of the porch. I had the feeling of being part of a great movement of man toward his door, as the whole countryside waited for those few drops to increase. Plop . . . plop . . . plop . . . They were hitting the ground vertically with a force that sent up little dry puffs of chalk. Plop . . . plop . . . plop, plop, plop, plop, plop—and the deluge came down in a flood of healing. I went out of the house and stood in that blessed rain until I could feel the little streams of water running down my skin.

Fred and the children came in from their walk, laughing delightedly. They were sleek with rain when they reached the porch.

"You should have been with us," said Fred. "Any dry clothes around?"

"I don't want to change." said Judy. "It feels so good."

"Better not take any chances of getting a cold," cautioned her father. "There'll be plenty of rain from now on."

The children called us early the next morning to see the miracle in our side yard. It was still raining. What had been the dry, gravely level between our house and the cook's quarters was now dotted with small, pink lilies which had sprung up and blossomed overnight—rain lilies, Taj called them. Over one night, the world had become green, lush, unbelievably beautiful.

People had changed, too. Though nothing had been said, and though no one showed any quick temper, there had been a brittle tension in the air as day after day the long drought built itself up. Now there was laughter everywhere. Tension had dripped off our fingers with the rain.

From then on, the monsoon continued the rest of the summer. Occasionally we would be treated to a magnificent sunset, but those occasions were rare. There were things we didn't like about the rain. It was impossible to dry the laundry. Every home had sheets, dresses, towels, and underwear—and many had diapers— hanging in living room, dining room, and kitchen. Mold grew on everything. It covered our shoes, our books, our belts; it got into the framed pictures hanging on the walls. All these were minor inconveniences in comparison to the blessed relief the rain was bringing to our parched world.

Our house was about three-fourths of the way between Woodstock School and the top of the hill. As we sloshed up the path for our language study, we reveled in the pale feathery ferns covering the trunks and branches of the trees; the begonias of all colors growing out of the rocks; the soft moss we wanted to touch ever so gently with the palms of our hands.

At a curve in the path we took, there was a large silver-gray rock, its center hollowed out by ages of dripping water from the stones above. Each day it held its bowl brimful of rain—that rain so precious, now falling with such abandon. I had all I could do to keep from stooping down to dip my fingers in the holy water in a gesture of gratitude.

"Go ahead, do it," said Fred, when I got the courage to confess this to him. "The stooping will do you good."

By the time the monsoon was over, we had passed our language examinations.

The children were excited about going into boarding school. Most of their friends were already there, their parents having left for the plains a month or so earlier than we who were in the language school. I had to try to be as excited about the boarding as they were. It was not easy, and I am sure they were not fooled.

We packed their tin trunks and sent them off with coolies the morning we left for Ludhiana.

"It won't be forever," Fred consoled me. "There are only a couple of months more before they'll be home for the long winter vacation. And you know how fast these months have gone."

"You'll have a wonderful time in boarding," I told the children. "There are only a couple of months more before you'll be home for the long winter vacation. And you know how fast these past months have gone."

The Ludhiana station platform looked like an Arabian Nights

version of the Garden of the Sleeping Beauty. We had taken the wrong train, and had arrived in Ludhiana an hour before we were expected. We had wired ahead that we were not to be met. (It seemed as if all trains arrived in Ludhiana before dawn—at least, all trains that had to be met.) During one long weekend break from language study, while we were still at Landour, Fred had made a trip to Bombay to pick up our freight. When he stopped off at Ludhiana with it, he had an overwhelming welcome from large numbers of the staff who were at the railway station at that early hour to greet him. There was no reason to repeat the performance today.

We picked our way between the sleeping figures—whole families had spread their bedding rolls on the cement platform. Coverings ranged from elaborately embroidered Kashmir shawls to ragged burlap. Many of the heads appearing above the covers were turbaned with bright-colored silks or cottons. Women's heads showed everything from sleek coiffeurs to tangled mats. Here and there a knee was visible, revealing the lovely turquoise, pink, or deep blue of what I called Scheherazade trousers—the voluminous pajama trousers of the Punjabi woman. She wears a long tunic over this, draped at the shoulders with a chiffon or gauze scarf.

Our footsteps echoed through the tin-roofed platforms, and I was sure the sleeping figures would waken; but they all slept heavily. A long-bearded, blue-turbaned pedicab driver woke up enough to help us with our luggage, and lead us to his vehicle.

Whoever designed Indian pedicabs had a grudge against people. It must have taken years of study to devise the cab so that every single part of it hit you in the wrong places; pitched you forward to that delicate balance where you were sure you were going to be catapulted into the street, but never were. Perhaps its designer was a pedicab *driver*, for the bicycle part of this ricksha looked

35

comfortable enough. Our driver gave a prodigious yawn, threw a leg over the shaft, braced himself erect on the pedals, and we were off.

Fred and I alternated at trying different pronunciations of our destination, including "Chreestian Madicul Colch." We were taken to the wrong place twice before our driver understood us. Then, "Ah! Brown Hospital!" he beamed. He pronounced it "Br-r-roon." We might have known, from all we had heard of her, that the name of Dr. Edith Brown would be associated with the institution which this English woman had founded. Whenever *she* arrived at this railway station, the people of the town met her with uniformed bands, armfuls of flowers, and an elephant to ride upon as the triumphal procession made its way along these very streets.

No music, no shouts of welcome echoed now—no sound at all

except the occasional ring of the pedicab bell. It looked as if all the people in town had bitten off chunks of the Sleeping Beauty's apple. Wooden cots with woven rope bottoms had been pulled out of the stifling houses; the sidewalks were lined on either side with sleeping families.

When we reached the gate of the residence compound, Fred saw that he knew the way from his previous visit. He paid the driver, and just as the world began to turn in its sleep, we entered a garden. The signs on the two brick pillars at the entrance assured me that I was not living in a fairy tale. UNITED CHURCH OF NORTHERN INDIA and EWING CHRISTIAN SCHOOL, they read.

Through the thick foliage of flowering trees, bright green parrots were flying. Our footsteps made no sound on the paths of golden sand. The dark red brick of the church loomed up in silence at our right, and on the left, an empty house stood among misty shrubs.

"Is this one our house?" I almost whispered it.

My husband boomed out, "No, that's where the Carl Taylors live. They are still on vacation. Ours is the one you see further to the left; you can just make it out at the end of this path."

The spell was broken; I was on solid earth again.

"But we turn to the right here," Fred added, taking my arm. "We have to pick up the keys from Mildred. Straight ahead is Mildred's school. Whoops, she doesn't like to have me call it that. Anyway, you know what I mean—Ewing Christian School."

As we walked along the path to Mildred's house, Fred continued to point things out. The Roys' house. He was the Indian pastor who was executive secretary of the Punjab Mission. "Our new boss," said Fred. "You'll meet him later. The Roys are a wonderful family. And in that house lives another great bunch of people—the Sardar Khans. Now you know the whole compound. Here we are at Mildred's."

"Mildred" was Mildred Hoffmeister, a quiet-voiced Texan of

37

about my age, I judged. Beside her was a honey-colored cocker named, well, Texas. Mildred's home was tastefully arranged, and looked the most like the United States of anything I'd seen in a long time.

We sat down to scrambled eggs, homemade bread toasted, quince jelly, coffee, and fruit. During breakfast we met most of the teachers from Ewing Christian School, who came in and out of the house informally. How so few of them managed to teach seven hundred and fifty boys and girls between the ages of four and eleven was more than I could fathom. We learned that they also taught in the Sunday School and were leaders in the Women's Group at church.

We were introduced to the gardener who was passing through the dining room carrying a woven rope bed. He was followed by one of the teachers with a child in her arms.

"Texas, go play with Kiran," said Mildred to her cocker, who was being fed pieces of toast and jelly. "Kiran hasn't been feeling well," Mildred told us. "I thought it would be cooler for the child under the fan in the living room than in the dormitory." (She called it "dawmitory.")

Mildred's home, we were to learn, was conference center, infirmary, youth hostel, rest home, orchestra pit, chapel, and inn. In it, I was to spend many restful (and later, creative) hours. Nor did I dream, that morning, that our last weeks in Ludhiana would be spent in these rooms.

The gateman arrived with a note which Mildred read with a smile. "The medical college folks say that I'm not to wait breakfast for you any longer. They've been down to the train to meet you and you weren't on it. Apparently you aren't coming today."

"But we wired them not to meet us," said Fred.

"Oh, that wouldn't make any difference to those folks," said Mildred.

Just then the school bell rang.

"There goes the bell; I'll have to leave," said Mildred. "I wanted to take you down to the house, but it's time for staff prayers. Here are the keys. I'll expect you for lunch at twelve, and for as many meals as you want to eat here until you get settled."

We thanked her, and hurried down the path to our new home.

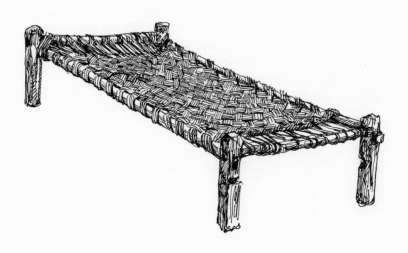

chapter six

As we emerged from the trees into the clearing on which the house stood, I was appalled. The house was round, and it was huge. Circular verandas downstairs, upstairs, and around the roof, made it look like a giant cake which had fallen—a very dirty cake at that. I hadn't been in India long enough to realize how quickly the jungle takes over. The house had been empty only a matter of months. The front porch was piled deep with debris from the large birds' nests over the front door. Cobwebs hung in festoons across the doors and windows. The place looked like one of those ghoulish cartoons in the *New Yorker*, only it wasn't very funny.

Chandru's wife, Umda appeared from the servants' quarters. Like the small deer of her hill country, she moved without sound. Chandru had sent home for her when he knew we would want him in Ludhiana. I was diverted for a moment, fascinated by her jewelry. The outer ridges of her ears were edged with large hoops of silver, so heavy that her ears were doubled over toward her face.

"Dirty, dirty," whispered Umda. She shook her head sadly and went back to help Chandru unpack.

Inside the house was just as bad. The rooms looked like deep, dark wells. (The ceilings were twenty-two feet high.) The window ledges had an inch or more of dried mud where the rains had flooded in. The floors, what we could see of them, were of rough cement. Furniture belonging to three families was stacked from floor half-way to ceiling in many of the rooms. In the dining room, our packing boxes all but blocked one entrance. And the bathrooms!

"Let's get to work," said Fred.

He opened his brief case, got out the tools and began to uncrate our boxes.

Let's get to work! I wandered from room to room, exhausted at the thought. At one end of the living room, there was a stained, broken-springed couch. I sank down on it. Before me, two long windows gave access to the front veranda. They were barred with heavy iron bars, set half an inch apart. Why, all the windows were barred! I felt trapped. Since our time in the concentration camp in China, claustrophobia had ceased to be a strange word in a nurse's textbook; it had become a frightening reality. I wanted to run, and I was too weak to run.

"Oh, God," I prayed, "I can't do it. I can't make a home of this house. And I can't tell Fred. He'd be so disappointed in me. What shall I do?"

I lay down and buried my face into the dusty back of the couch so Fred would not hear me crying. Then I heard his voice above me.

"Pretty awful, isn't it?" he said.

He sat down on the couch, lifted me up, and put his arms around me. "Go ahead, cry," he said.

I reached for his handkerchief. A fine "tower of strength" I was being! I'd come out to India to help him, not to hang like a dead albatross around his neck.

As I dried my eyes, I thought I saw a fireplace behind two piled-up tables. "I've always wanted a fireplace," I said. "And is there any way we can get the bars off those windows?"

Later, when the place was clean, the bars removed, the draperies and large pictures hung, the Chinese rug laid, the furniture polished and spread out through the house, the bowls of flowers arranged, I knew we had a home, and I was extremely grateful to God for once more seeing me through. I wondered why I hadn't seen at once the possibilities of this delightful hundred-year-old house.

Fred couldn't wait to show me the hospital where he would be working. He had seen it all on his previous visit, and wanted me to take the tour at once.

Dr. Eileen Snow, the Director of the Medical College and Hospital, showed us through the afternoon we arrived in Ludhiana. We met her at her rooms in the administration building of the medical college compound. It was a lovely old rambling structure a few steps back from the chapel, which was just inside the front gate. The buildings were painted a dark red with white trim.

"They call this place Lal Khoti," said Fred. "It has a living room, dining room, and sleeping rooms for the staff's unappropriated blessings," he added, using his name for unmarried women.

Dr. Snow came down the steps from her vine-covered veranda to greet us. Eileen P. Barter Snow was from England (as were many on the staff). I liked her at once, and we became very close friends. She had eyes the color of forget-me-nots, a smile that suddenly twinkled over her otherwise calm face, and a quiet dignity that was somehow very British.

43

After we had been introduced, she said to Fred, "We'll show her the medical college another day. Let's take her to the hospital first."

We went out the front gate, crossed Brown Road, and walked down it until we came to the hospital on our right. It was a veritable rabbit warren of one-story buildings, branching off in every direction except up and down. It was certainly an old structure, but the rooms were clean. Fresh paint or whitewash covered the cracked walls; pictures had been hung, and flowers arranged in empty ink bottles painted dark green.

We went first to the wards where Fred would be working. Remembering the mud walls and thatched roofs of our first hospital in China, I was not as shocked as I might have been. Remembering, too, the compact, efficient, sixty-bed hospital Fred had built there, I knew that these dark, meandering, crowded buildings would soon be changed. This was one of the reasons why Fred had been chosen for this post.

Dr. Snow read my thoughts. "Now you see why we are so glad you have come," she said. "And why we've all been working so hard for the new hospital. As you can see, we need you very much, Doctor Scovel."

We made slow progress through the hospital courtyards. An Indian student nurse, in crisp blue and white, approached with a chart in her hand. Dr. Snow asked a few questions and wrote an order. A workman wanted to know where to open another door into a ward. A student wanted an appointment to talk over a family problem. A young woman, disheveled, and wearing a dirty cotton sari, dropped to her knees and touched Dr. Snow's feet in gratitude. Dr. Snow took her by the arm and lifted her up. "Don't thank me, thank God," she said. Then to us, "As many years as I've been in India, it still embarrasses me terribly when patients do that." An old lady in a very clean white sari had mischief in her eyes; she had evidently stopped Dr. Snow to

45

tell her a joke. Dr. Snow quipped back in Urdu, then introduced us.

"That little woman is the matriarch in a family of goldsmiths," said Dr. Snow as we entered the sterilizing room off the operating theater. "She is a Hindu, but she loves this hospital; she comes often to give voluntary service here.

"I suppose you are wondering why in the world anyone ever built a hospital like this in the first place." Dr. Snow again read my thoughts. "You see, this hospital used to be what we call a *purdah* hospital. It was built in the days when women were kept in strict seclusion; each room had to have an access to the street so that the man in the family could come in to see his wife or mother without seeing, or being seen by, the other women in the hospital. As the hospital expanded, you can see for yourself what happened—a wing here, another over there, and so it grew."

We continued on, seeing the maternity ward and the nursery. The chubby, bronze-colored, round-eyed babies made it difficult to go on to the men's surgical wing.

"How long has it been a men's hospital, too?" I asked.

A deep shadow crossed Dr. Snow's face, and she said, very quietly, "Ever since the riots in 1947, when India and Pakistan became divided. The slaughter was terrible . . . unbelievable, really, when a moment before we had all lived together so peaceably. We took in everyone—men, women, Hindus, Muslims, and Sikhs. . . ." She straightened her shoulders and added brightly, "You'll be wanting your tea. We'll go back to my room. You've seen enough for one afternoon."

The heat hit us like the opening of an oven door when we stepped out into the road from the shelter of the thick-walled buildings. We squeezed between ricksha pedicabs, snorting trucks, and a herd of water buffaloes just coming in from grazing. As one of the buffaloes was in the act of defecating, two children ran into the road, jostling each other and cupping their hands to

LUDHIANA SUBURB

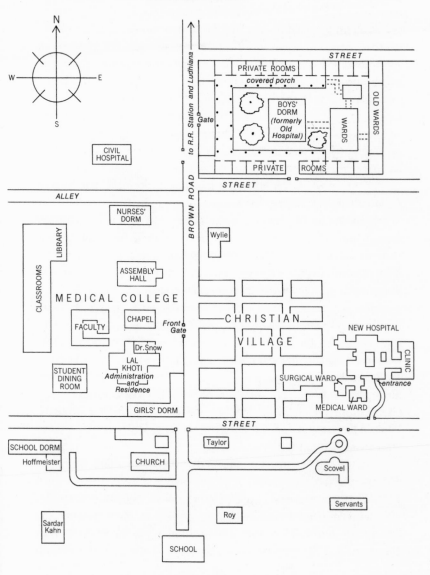

get the precious cow dung to dry for fuel cakes. I tried my best not to be shocked; this was one of the normal sights I'd have to get used to. Fred didn't bat an eye; but he took my hand as we went through the medical college gate, then quickly dropped it, remembering that here, as in China, husbands and wives did not touch one another in public. There was so much to remember— so much new to learn.

As we drank our tea in Dr. Snow's living room, she told us of the beginnings of the medical college, and of Dame Edith Brown, its founder.

"'Dame' must have a different meaning in English than it does in American," said Fred. "What *does* it mean in English?"

"It is an honor conferred by the British Government," said Dr. Snow. "For her work in India, King George V honored Doctor Brown with the title, Dame Commander of the British Empire. That was in 1931, I believe. The investiture took place in the Throne Room of the Viceroy's residence in Delhi."

"Then it certainly doesn't mean the same as in American," said Fred. "It is—well, it's slang for a girl," he hastily added to answer the question in Dr. Snow's raised eyebrow. "Tell us more. How long ago was the medical college founded."

"Dame Edith opened it on January 4, 1894. It was the first medical college for women in all of Asia. She began it with four Christian girls as medical students, and two as dispenser students. Her whole capital for the enterprise was the gift of a personal friend—fifty pounds."

"That would be about a hundred and forty dollars, wouldn't it?" asked Fred.

"About that. I'm never sure of those things," Dr. Snow replied. "Certainly not much with which to begin a medical college; but Doctor Brown had an idea, and insisted upon carrying it out. The first anatomy dissection room was a latrine. And to think

that now we have two hundred and fifty students, fourteen mission agencies co-operating, and will one day have a new five-hundred-bed hospital—all in one woman's lifetime!"

"Is Doctor Brown still living?" I asked.

"Yes, she is living on a houseboat in Kashmir," said Dr. Snow. "She keeps well, but is getting more feeble all the time. She is over ninety."

"We mustn't keep you from your work any longer," said Fred. "It's been a wonderful afternoon. I can't wait to get started."

"You'd better take a few more days to get settled," said Dr. Snow as we said goodbye.

chapter seven

Was there the proverbial quiet at the core of the maelstrom of work into which we were suddenly thrown? If so, we were caught in the swirl too far from the center to find it.

Fred was, to use the Indian expression, *"nak tuk,* up to the nose," in outpatient clinics, ward rounds, teaching rounds, patients, patients, patients. His class for the students on internal medicine entailed, we figured, about fifteen hours of preparation for each hour in the classroom. "It will be easier as time goes on," he said.

Fred had been appointed superintendent of the hospital; he carried on in this capacity for a year or more, all the time on the lookout for some Indian doctor on the staff who might take his place. He was delighted when the Board of Governors appointed Dr. Ram Singh. This white-haired gentleman looked, and was, every inch the benevolent Christian physician.

Added to his usual activities, Fred had the job of setting up his department. "There isn't one single thing now as I want it to be," he said as he came in for lunch one mid-afternoon.

In order that his students could study cases, hospital records had to be dug out of a storeroom, numbered and catalogued according to the World Health Organization's nomenclature of disease. He did this late at night, after he had prepared his lectures —except on the nights when the building committee met.

Fred was chairman of this committee for the building of the new hospital. He would come home from those meetings completely exhausted, only to have two members of the staff drop in later to argue, question, and oppose all that was being done.

Years ago, we had heard Dr. E. M. Dodd, Medical Secretary of the Presbyterian Board of Foreign Missions, tell a group of candidates, "We hardly expect you missionaries to get along well together. We have chosen you because you are leaders, and you all know what happens when a bunch of Mussolinis get together."

Ned Dodd knew, and we soon learned, that underneath any bickering there was a deep and abiding affection which no amount of disagreement on policy ever touched. But there were nights, as I lay in bed listening to the insistent voices, and Fred's tired replies, when I could have taken those two staff members and bashed their heads together.

Our group was further complicated by our being from many different countries and denominations. We differed in teaching methods, on hospital techniques, modes of discipline and administration. Some were the only representatives of their denominations, which meant that they were responsible to headquarters if things in the building or administration were not in accord with their particular policy. And the day was past when "the Board" sat in far-off New York or London and knew little of what was going on. We had a constant flow of mission executives from all over the world, each one given the red-carpet treatment, and each one with his own idea of where hallway, ward, cupboard, and equipment should be placed. Nursing staff and medical staff did not agree. (I was on the side of the nurses.)

The architect, a talented young man just out from England, bit the stem of his Sherlock Holmes pipe, and quietly went mad. But at last his plans were approved, and he returned joyfully to England.

It was time to decide on letting the contract. There was enough money on hand to complete the main building, an outpatient department, operating rooms, pharmacy, and three hundred and fifty of the five hundred beds. Money would have to be raised for the X-ray department, pathology, maternity, and private-patients wings. Hopefully it would come in before the first part of the building was finished. If the money did not come in, it would mean letting another contract later, buying building supplies in two lots, and thus at higher rates. Should the contract be let *before* there was enough money on hand to pay for everything planned?

Dr. Carl Taylor, one of the other Presbyterian doctors on the staff, said no. Carl was doing a tremendous job, recognized by the India Medical Council as the most effective way of teaching public health to medical students, by village living. (Two students, one Punjabi-speaking, were assigned to each family, and were expected to help them in all Public Health problems. During this time, the students learned the true needs of the villagers, and that there is more to healing than the textbook treatment of a disease.)

Carl was a clear thinker, excellent at long-range planning—a man whose opinion was valuable. He argued, and many agreed, that one does not build without first sitting down and counting the cost. Then he builds according to what he has on hand. Suppose that giving did not come up to our expectations. We would be showing poor stewardship with what we had if we began and could not finish. The money already given had been raised with great effort—a trust from individuals who believed in us. (One girl in Australia had picked up empty Coke bottles from the

53

streets and redeemed them for her offering.) Carl, and those staff members who agreed with him, were right, and Fred knew they were right.

On the other hand, those staff members who had been with the institution for a much longer time, insisted that unless we were going to trust God, and go ahead in faith, we were never going to have a hospital. When the Indian government decreed that the college should upgrade, and made the building of a new hospital one of the requirements, the little band of women staff members had a decision to make. They had to decide whether the medical college, then giving only the licentiate degree, should close, or upgrade to meet the difficult standards required to give the M.B.B.S. degree. They had practically no money at all; the funds needed were overwhelming. These women had gone to their knees in prayer. When they arose, they did so with the complete assurance that God would provide for each step of the way.

Dr. Eileen Snow had gone around the world; had interested individuals and mission boards to give money and provide staff. Now, miraculously, there was enough money on hand for the first phase. Should we not begin to build in faith that money to complete it would come in? These colleagues were right, and Fred knew they were right. He felt trapped between the two approaches.

The building committee met longer than usual on the night that the decision was to be made. It was after midnight when Fred came upstairs.

"How did it go?" I asked.

"You should be asleep," he said. "We couldn't come to any decision. It sure is a tough one to make."

He wound his watch and set it on the dresser, then sat down in the creaky little rocker to untie his shoelaces. "Well, we can't do it both ways," he said with a sigh. "We'll have to find out what God wants us to do. We are all going to pray tonight and tomorrow; then meet again tomorrow night."

He was still on his knees when I fell asleep.

I knew that the impasse had been resolved when he came in early the next evening.

"We've done it!" he said, his old boyish enthusiasm back again. "For better or for worse, we've done it! And the decision to sign the contract was unanimous. It gives you the feeling of being part of destiny."

The building site was across the road from our house. We went over every day to see how the work was progressing. It was thrilling to see the foundations dug so that the floor plan was laid out on the ground before us. Then the piles of red brick appeared, and at last a flurry of activity—men and women running

up and down planks, carrying bricks, mortar, and goatskins filled with water. The women workers were as strong as the men, though graceful in their bright-colored, full skirts. The silver of their earrings, bracelets, and anklets, contrasted with the bronze of their skin. The reds, blues, greens, and yellows of the men's turbans added to the "spectacular" going on before our eyes.

The leading characters in the drama were being played by a new English architect who had come out to carry on with the actual building, a handsome young Indian architect, and the brothers Singh, the contractors, who were Sikhs. One of the brothers was an intense executive with iron-gray hair; the other was short, and very round, with a long white beard. He reminded me of a jovial King of the Golden River.

There were many headaches behind the production of the scene taking place across the street from us. The building committee still met late, night after night, as the staff and the new architect fought through round after weary round. Fred groaned in his sleep, quivered and tossed.

One afternoon as we were having our coffee on the lawn (it was too cold in the house heated only by fireplaces), Eileen Snow stopped by. Her face was drawn and her voice hoarse with weariness. She dropped into a chair, and I poured her a cup of coffee. She and Fred were soon deep in the discussion of a peculiarly knotty problem: what to do now that the steel strike was on in India.

Eileen suddenly turned to me. "Myra," she said, "do you believe in a personal devil? He seems intent upon blocking everything we're trying to do."

"That's because you're doing such a good job," I assured her. "Otherwise he wouldn't be the slightest bit interested."

chapter eight

Yes, I believed in a personal devil. I was having a bout with him. One thing about living in India for which I was totally unprepared, was the influx of visitors who took over my home. In fact, it was no longer a home; it was an inn.

While in Landour, we had heard something about this. We knew that Ludhiana was a center to which missionaries came for necessary shopping, for medical treatment and their required annual physical examinations. Too, the medical college drew visitors from all over the world. We knew that we would be called upon to do our share of the entertaining. This we had always delighted in doing.

What we didn't know was that in this land of open hospitality, people rarely troubled to let you know they were coming. My first encounter with the situation came one day when I arrived home for lunch after a very busy morning in my new capacity as medical college librarian. One of our fellow missionaries, Ernie

Campbell from Jullundur, and a man in United States Government Service, had arrived, told the cook they wanted hot water for baths, and were unpacking in the rooms I had just finished settling for our children. Ernie came out of the bedroom to greet me, all enthusiasm.

He wasn't deceived in the least by my forced cordiality. My cool reception puzzled this man whose own heart and home were open to the whole world, as I soon learned. In fact, I so unnerved him that he spilled the cup of coffee he was holding, and this made him even more nervous.

Ernie sat down in the rocker, and tactfully set me straight on what was expected of a woman in the Punjab. There was no other place for people to stay, no suitable hotels in town. This was the accepted pattern. We would be staying in homes wherever we traveled in India, either with missionaries or with Indian friends.

"Wasn't it like this in China?" asked Ernie, suddenly getting out of his chair and pacing the room.

"It probably was in the larger centers," I said, remembering how long I had stayed with friends in Tsinan when my babies had been born. "But we lived in the interior and nobody ever came to see us. Have some more coffee."

"Thanks. I think the record for this house was made one weekend when the Bill Barrs lived here," he said. "There was a wedding in town, and they had seventy-two guests between Thursday and Monday."

Ernie never gave any evidence that he held against me his first stay in our home. And his beautiful blonde wife taught me many things about how to be a gracious hostess easily in this country to which I had come. (The definition which a few of us wives secretly passed around was that a gracious hostess is one who makes her guest feel at home when she wishes he were.)

I was losing my bout with the devil because of deep resentment over the situation. I was so very busy. My work at the library was

60

difficult. The only thing I knew about a library was that books had white numbers written on their backs. But there was no one else who had the time to take care of the library, so I would have to learn.

"Isn't there some key to this—some system or other?" I had asked the librarian who was retiring.

"We used to have a typewritten booklet, but it got lost," she replied.

"You'll have to write home for the Dewey Decimal System," was Fred's advice. Now, with the help of Doris Crawford, librarian teacher from our mission in Allahabad, and Sara Hazlett, ex-librarian, now in Dehra Dun, who spent a week at my side, complete chaos was beginning to give way to order.

I would rush home from the confusion of the library to the confusion of five unexpected guests, three of whom would like to eat at once because they had appointments at the hospital, and two of whom had gone to the bazaar and wouldn't be back for another hour.

Chandru served meals at nine different times one day. It was nothing to have forty-eight napkins in the wash. (Paper ones were far too expensive to use.) We never knew how much food to buy. Nearly everyone paid for meals and lodging, but this only added to my frustration. I wanted to be a hostess in my own home —not a hotel manager.

The devil almost had me pinned to the mat. These constant comings and goings were hard on Fred. When he came home in the evening, he wanted to sit down with his pipe and a book to relax for a while before he went into his study for his evening work. As it was now, he spent that precious time being sociable.

Was this what God had called me to India to do?

At least, this was the job He was giving me to do at the moment, and I did not like it.

One afternoon I went up to lie on the woven rope bed on the

upstairs porch. I had to come to grips with this problem and could do it better lying down. The Chinaberry tree smelled like the lilacs in Stony Point.

I had come to love this garden, this home. I had not dreamed, when I gave up our Stony Point home so reluctantly, that I would so quickly transplant my roots into Indian soil. But I wanted to keep this place all to ourselves. I wanted to invite our friends to visit us at *our* convenience. We had had such a good time the other night with our Indian Pastor, Amos Boyd and his family. I had wanted to invite the Roys the following week, but who knew how many would appear at our table the night I planned it? Daisy and Taj came in often, because they were teaching us language every day and knew exactly what was going on. We loved having them run in with a bowl of greens and corn bread, to have an unexpected lunch with us.

There was so much I wanted to do. I wanted long hours over coffee with Ruth Bergevin on poetry; or with Gertrude Nyce on the Christian Family devotional book I was writing; or with Ernestine Sauer on chit-chat about our children in America. I wanted my home to be my castle, inviolate, with the drawbridge pulled up when I wanted to pull it up.

For some reason, I thought of a story we had heard of one of our missionaries in Japan. Perhaps it was because *her* home had burned down. She had been out on a preaching tour in the country, and had returned to find the house and all her possessions in ashes. As she stood there, stunned, a Japanese friend came across the fields carrying a small silver vase. It had belonged to the missionary's mother.

"Some time before this, my Japanese friend had been ill," the missionary had said. "The first rose had blossomed in my garden, and I wanted to take it to her. I debated whether or not to put the rose in my precious silver vase. At last, I did, and took it across to my sick friend. So you see, what I kept, I lost; and what I gave away, I kept."

This was the key. If I wanted this home, I'd have to give it up. Certainly I was not enjoying it now. It was eating out my insides. Why had it been so much easier to brave machine-gun fire in China, than it was to chase out these "little foxes" which were destroying the vines?

The children from Ewing School were coming down the path. It was time for their singing lesson. I would enjoy every minute of them without worrying that dear Ruth Morgan, in bed with a sinus infection, might be wakened from a nap; or that Bill, her red-headed husband, would not be able to study for his language examination for another half hour. I gave back to God the house and all its occupants, present and future. By the time Christmas came, I could welcome the Christ Child with Open House. My adversary retired, panting, to his corner.

But before Christmas was "Going Down Day"—the day on which Woodstock School closed, and the children "went down" the mountain to disperse to their homes on the plains of India and to some twelve countries of the world. It was too cold, and there was too much snow in those Himalayan foothills to continue through the winter, so the long vacation of the school year was from the last of November until the first of March. School remained in session all summer, and the parents of the students went to Landour for their vacation to be with their children.

The trainload of Woodstock young people was due to arrive in Ludhiana at 3:21 A.M. We parents were gathered on the station platform, shivering with cold or excitement, or both. Many of us seldom met except on this occasion, and the pleasant reunion helped to pass the time.

There was Major Myadas from Ferozepore. I was never quite sure of his title. He used to tell me I raised his rank each time we met. He was a fine Indian gentleman, a fruit grower whose acres, handed down in his family for generations, had been much improved by him. Once a year, he and his wife and her sister would

drive down from Ferozepore to bring us some delicious grape-
fruit from their trees. The Myadases were one of the first Christian families in that part of the Punjab. Their son, Ashok, was
in Tom's class.

Then there was the very beautiful Mrs. Mehra and her husband,
a fellow Rotarian of Fred's. The Mehras' rose gardens were sheer
delight to us when we attended an occasional tea party in them.
They had a son in the class below Judy's.

And there were Mr. and Mrs. Raikhy, whose son, Anil, was
in Judy's class. We had first met the Raikhys through his being
a patient of Fred's. Mr. Raikhy loved being outdoors, and though
he was the owner of one of Ludhiana's largest cinemas, he spent
most of his time in the country. He would stop by on his way
into the city on his motorcycle, always with some gift for us.

Besides the missionaries who had come in from surrounding

areas to pick up their children, there were the Americans who were working on the Bakra Dam at nearby Nangal.

As the time stretched on, we became more and more quiet. Would the train never come? The station again took on its Arabian Nights quality. All the colors we were wearing were changed by the alchemy of the hour and the strange neon lights overhead. My red coat became a deep purple. Fred, who had gone to see why the train was late, was running down the steps of the overhead crossing. Had there been a wreck? No. He had been told by the stationmaster that the engine was in sight.

Suddenly, the floor we were standing on rattled and shook, the train shrieked in, and disgorged its load of some two hundred children onto the platform. Most of them would be going on to further destinations, but they all had to say goodbye to their friends, play a little catchball, or buy tea and samosas (a meat-filled pastry). Screams of delight at the finding of parents, or shouts of recognition to the parents of friends, transformed the staid old station into a campus on the last day of school.

I was suddenly hugged by two pairs of arms at once. In an embrace of soft necks, sooty cheeks, and hair stiff with the dust of the trip, my contented mother-feeling returned. My children were home for Christmas!

We sorted out the trunks, found our pedicab rickshas, left the crowd still shouting, and drove home through the early dawn to cocoa and toast, baths and bed.

chapter nine

"Come on, Vicki. Time to run the mile. I've got it paced off."
Tom had his plans all made for the girls' vacation.

"Oh, Tommy, I'm too tired," Vicki replied. "I'll do it this
afternoon."

"This afternoon, nothing," Tom insisted. "Judy's just finished
the broad jump. Let's see if you can break your yesterday's record."

Loath as the girls were to do anything that smacked of physical
exercise, they always went through their paces for Tom. And all
three worked with me in the library.

Christmas preparations were fitted in happily whenever we
could manage it. Gifts for our family in America had been purchased during the summer and shipped home early in October.
Christmas cards went out in early November. The two girls and

I would have to make three or four trips to the bazaar to finish the last minute buying. We loved those narrow, stone-rutted streets off the main thoroughfare, where the little shops shouldered their way nearer and nearer to the center of the road. The shop-keepers sat on green baize carpets high enough from the street so that shoppers were on eye level with them.

This morning the yards of gold and silver ribbon fell into the storekeeper's voluminous white lap. We would buy kite paper for gift wrappings at a shop farther on, not far from where Vicki had gone to buy brass bells for Judy's ankles. (Both girls were taking lessons in Indian classical dancing.)

"I need sequins," said Judy. "How do you say it in Hindustani?"

"I don't know, but I'll try something," I replied. "What in the world do you want sequins for?"

"Don't ask questions," said Judy. "It's Christmas. Remember?"

I turned to the shopkeeper. "We want the little *tikas* women paste between their eyebrows," I ventured. "Only these have two little holes in them, and are sometimes sewn around the borders of saris."

He turned to his helper with, "Sequins *mujhe de dou*," ("Give me the sequins"), "sequins" being the only *English* word he used!

Once the gifts were bought, we were ready to begin final prep-arations for the Christmas parties.

We wanted our celebrations to commemorate the coming of the Child who was the Light of the world. Some of the Christians here in Ludhiana would be outlining their homes with little oil lamps to show their neighbors that the coming of that Light meant something very important in their lives. Other Christians would shun the custom as being too reminiscent of the Hindu Divali Festival.

The center of our family Christmas had always been the creche. On the Sunday before Christmas, when I began the annual reading aloud of Dickens' *A Christmas Carol*, we made a little service of

68

arranging on the mantle the beautiful German figures which Grandmother had bought for us years ago in Tsingtao, China. Vicki especially liked to arrange the figures of the animals around the manger. One little lamb had to be placed so that its nose was in the Christ Child's outstretched hand.

But we also wanted a lighted Christmas tree to recall the happy memories of our own tradition. After my efforts to get this across to the gardener, I almost gave up.

"You mean you want this tree dug up?" he asked, as he shifted his soiled white turban with both hands, holding the trowel which he never set down. I sometimes wondered if it had become part of his right hand. "What's wrong with leaving it where it is? It is doing very well here. Arborvitae trees don't like to be moved."

"I know, but you can dig it up very carefully and plant it in this box," I tried to explain.

"You want this tree planted in a box? Why?" His usually dead-pan face now showed his annoyance.

"You want to put it into the house? At the end of the living room?" He was sure that he had not understood me.

"Well, you see, we are going to hang ornaments on it . . ." I finally gave up trying to explain.

He argued, he protested, he groaned as I insisted. He knew I was completely out of my mind—bringing a tree into the house. Humph! He all but convinced me that he was correct in his assumption. If the girls hadn't been sorting out the old decorations and making new ones, I would have succumbed to his pleading.

And the tree did look beautiful, hung with strings of popcorn (we had brought a can from America for this very occasion); decorated with garlands made from the brightly colored brushes used to whirl the mud off ricksha wheels, gold-paper pictures, Santa's boots made by the children when they were small, and a few shining balls and lights we had saved over the years. When I saw how the staff members enjoyed it, I was glad I had not given in.

We had asked about the usual senior-staff festivities, and found that the women at Lal Khoti gave themselves so completely to others during Christmas week that they had little or no celebration for themselves. We decided to give them a Christmas party in our home, and in the end we invited the whole senior staff—Americans from the United States, Canadians, English, Scots, Germans, Australians, Irish, Indians. Those who had wives or husbands brought them along. That first year we sent out sixty-two invitations, but as the hospital grew and the staff increased, we had nearer one hundred and twenty-five in subsequent years.

How grateful we were for our large house! We pushed back beds to make couches in corners, decorated dressers to look like tables, opened double doors to allow a flow of movement, and lit fires in all four fireplaces.

Expense was shared by the married couples who brought candy, nuts, and the Christmas cakes, pies, or cookies which were traditional in their own countries or families. Judy, Vicki, Chandru, and I baked fruit cake, made popcorn balls, and prepared the coffee, tea, and hot spiced orange juice.

Promptly at eight o'clock, the guests began to arrive. The men wore black business suits or tuxedos; the women wore long evening dresses. One could easily judge the number of years of service of the wearer, as we usually made one evening dress give a lifetime of service. I obviated this age-giveaway by wearing a long black skirt given to me years before by an Australian friend in China; over it, a Chinese brocade jacket in red and gold. Seeing each other out of "uniform," and in such gala attire, set the tone for a happy evening.

After our coffee, everyone crowded into the living room where chairs had been set up in rows facing the fireplace. The Christmas tree stood resplendent at the right of it.

"And are we going to have charades?" one of the English women had asked when she received her invitation. She pronounced it "sharáds," and it took me a moment to understand

what she meant. My total experience with charades went back to my childhood, and acting out "Constant—Tie—Noble," the capital of Turkey. I wasn't prepared for her next sentence. "You'll be sure to let us know what group we are in, won't you? So we can prepare our costumes."

These charades were theatrical productions resulting in a display of talent we hadn't known existed in our usually sedate group. We laughed until we ached at imposing Sister Hanning explaining the Tower of London to her dumb students (an Indian professor, the Secretary to the Director, and the Head of the Pharmacy). We couldn't get our breath when quiet little Dr. Mary Eldrich portrayed Fred's six-foot-one at a committee meeting, his head on one side, his forefinger emphasizing a point.

There were games and there was Santa Claus, and there were gifts, and there were carols, including all verses of "The Twelve Days of Christmas" sung at gratifying speed. And there was our beloved Indian Padri in his best Punjabi suit, who led us in a

Christmas prayer for each other, for our work, and for those we loved "no matter where they may be."

After the goodnights had been said, Fred and I and the children stood on the veranda and watched the flashlights pouring warm pools of light along the sandy road and out into the black night.

I knew that the gardener had forgiven me for my folly over the Christmas tree when he came in on Christmas Eve to join in the service of worship we had with Chandru and his family. Mali (we called him by the Hindustani word for "gardener") brought in heavy garlands of marigolds and hung them around each of our necks.

Chandru's father was visiting us, and he read the Christmas story from Luke. Chandru led us in prayer, and Fred gave a little speech of gratitude for their help to us; saying that God had called each one of us in the room to a particular task, and that we could not do ours without their assistance. I passed out the gifts—some needed article of clothing and something completely frivolous for each one.

Then we all went into the dining room for a meal together. We sat on the floor, a tablecloth spread before us. Chandru had cooked the food. (He wouldn't trust me with it.) Tom, Judy, and Vicki waited on table between bites. Chandru and Balu had fun with the children. "A little more service here, Tommy. I'm out of tea." "Coming right up, Sir," Tom would reply. Umda made deprecating noises at Chandru for daring to talk to Tom in this way.

Before we had finished eating, the groups of carolers began to arrive. We were suddenly startled to hear one group singing loudly, "Home, Home on the Range." In trooped the entire Sardar Khan family—mother, father, grown sons, their wives, the grandchildren. They were all laughing. Sham Shad had a guitar.

"We thought we'd surprise you with a real American song," he said. "From the look on your faces, you *were* surprised."

Carolers came and went. There were groups of villagers singing their lilting, syncopated *bhajans*; there were teachers playing *sitars*; there were the medical students, their young faces lit by the candles they were holding. At last we could stay awake no longer, and the rest of the night we called "Merry Christmas" or the Hindustani equivalent, *"Bara Din Mubarik Ho*— Blessings on you, this Great Day," from the upstairs porch, snatching what sleep we could get between greetings.

The next morning, I was unwrapping a mysterious package which turned out to be a beautiful red tablecloth, whose embroidered Christmas trees Judy had covered with sequins. Someone knocked at the door. Fred put down Vicki's gift to him, a copy of *The Universe around Us*, and went out to see who it was. In a moment he was back.

"Come out here," he said to me. "I want you to meet a friend of mine."

At the door stood a wiry, gray-bearded man wearing a blue turban. His shirt was frayed, his short trousers faded and torn, his legs bare; and on his feet were crumpled Punjabi shoes. All this we took in at a quick glance, for we could not take our eyes off his radiant face. Fred had to bow very low as the man hung a garland of marigolds around his neck and placed a gift in Fred's hands.

Our overwhelming surprise and our gratitude seemed to please our guest; he walked away with a contented smile.

"Who is he?" I asked, when Fred returned from seeing him to the gate.

"Don't you know?" asked Fred. "He's the pedicab driver who takes me on out calls. It sure was nice of him to come on Christmas morning. He isn't a Christian; he's a Sikh, I think."

We opened the gift wonderingly. It was a framed picture of blind Hope with a broken harp, sitting on a cloud-covered world.

I wanted to run down the road after that dear man and hug him.

73

chapter ten

"Sorry I'm so late. You shouldn't have waited," said Fred one night as he came in to dinner. "I got held up. Another emergency. Poor old man with heart disease. I wanted to do an electrocardiogram on him."

"Are you sure you weren't just sitting there flirting with those good-looking medical students and nurses?" I asked.

"Not all nurses are as irresistible as you are," he quipped back. "Have a potato."

"No, thanks. I want to keep irresistible." I told him.

"You two make me sick," said Vicki. "You're too old to act this way."

"Some day, young lady, you will learn that a man is never too old to make love to a beautiful wife," said her father.

"Ssssh!" I said, quickly. "It's Tuesday night."

I had heard the rocking chair squeak. Kailash Mattur must have come in for the weekly meeting of our student group.

"We'll have our desert with them," I whispered. "I had Chandru get some *burfee*." (*Burfee* was an Indian sweet similar to divinity fudge with a slight cardomon flavor. The students loved it.)

We found Kailash in his favorite chair, his black curly head bent over a book he had picked up from the table. Soon the others began to come in: Jasbir Kaur, the lovely Sikh girl, the chiffon scarf of her Punjabi suit framing her earnest face; Bindra, a handsome Hindu, who wrote poetry, and who was so sure of himself it frightened me; Sylvia, the charming daughter of the Indian doctor who was Medical Director of Miraj Medical Centre; Dharm Dev, a little shy at first, but he later called me "Mama-Ji."

It was a good night—almost all the twenty-two were present.

The plan of the college was to divide the students into what were called "family groups" of about twenty students each. When a student entered the college, he (or she) was assigned to a group in which he remained as long as he had any connection with the institution. Thus we could get to know a few students more intimately than in the classroom; we could also be on the lookout for homesickness or trouble with examinations or the depression arising from an unhappy love affair!

There were always four or five staff members in each "family." Ours had Dr. Margaret Tucker, the radiologist whose parents we had known in China; Dr. Mukerji, a fine-looking young Indian physiologist from Calcutta, and Dr. Laker, a nervous, slight Anglo-Indian woman, to whom patients came from hundreds of miles away to have their eyes cared for. (Students could tell stories of her that would make the absent-minded professor look like a Roth memory expert.)

We took turns leading the discussions. Some years we had a series on "The Ethics of a Christian Doctor." Once we studied Paul Tournier's book, *A Doctor's Case Book in the Light of the Bible.* Often we studied a book of the Bible, though these students were not all Christians. It was often the other-than-Christians who suggested the Bible study.

76

Fred and I tried to learn as much as we could of the religions represented in our group. Of the Parsi's religion of Light, Zoroastrianism, we had already heard through stories of the three Wise Men who followed the star to Bethlehem. The ancestors of these students had come to Bombay from Persia in the eighth century.

Sikhism had been born in the Punjab at our very doors. The Sikhs believed in one God, renounced caste, eschewed idol worship, served others, and revered their holy book, the Granth. It had some very beautiful passages in it. "My path will be known to him who shares the fruit of his labors with others," one of today's Sikh leaders, the old saint Jodh Singh Sahib, once quoted to us.

We had no Muslims in our group. As for Hinduism, Fred and I read, we studied, and we listened, but we still do not know what Hinduism is. It is woven inextricably into the pattern of Indian culture. Three constants seem to be the belief in Karma (the cause and effect of actions on the growth of the soul), rebirth and transmigration (though we heard two Hindu students argue two totally different meanings to this concept), and caste. It was good for each of us to have to defend what we believed before those of other faiths.

We searched for ways to tell the students of the uniqueness of Christ. We soon found that the Bible spoke more convincingly than we did. Over the years we came to know that it was not so much what a missionary said, as what he was, that spoke to people about Christ. It put a frightening responsibility upon our shoulders, nor did it release us from the effort to speak out about our convictions when we were asked what we believed and why.

Tonight it was my turn to lead, and I was on the spot. "How can anyone know who is right?" asked Burkhat Masih, one of the Christian students. "We say one thing, somebody else says another. We can't both be right."

I looked helplessly at Fred.

"Tell them what Dr. Ram Singh said at the meeting of the Student Christian Movement," Fred helped me out.

"He told us it was like putting together a jigsaw puzzle," I began. "I am working in my corner, and all my pieces eventually fit together, except for a few on the outer edge that I don't know what to do with."

"I see what he means," said Bindra, warming to the metaphor. "We are all working at our separate bits of truth. Most of our pieces fit together, but we all have some left over that we don't know what to do with."

"Occasionally someone comes along, picks up a piece and fits it in for you, and after that a lot of pieces begin to fall into place," said Dhanawade, one of our Christian students from western India.

"That's it," I said. "But from where I am working, what you are doing in your corner doesn't make sense. And from where Bindra is working, what I am doing doesn't make sense."

"Oh, it isn't that bad," said Bindra, and we all laughed.

Dr. Mukerji had been edging forward on his chair. "But don't you see?" he said, "The key figure is missing. We are all working at *edge* pieces. We need something tangible, the figure of a person to hold all the bits together. For me, that person is Jesus Christ, who cared enough to give his life to show us how to fit the pieces together."

"Truth is truth, and must be whole, even though we can't see that it is whole," said Fred. "The trouble is that none of us, including all of us who are Christians, puts that Person in the center. We are always trying to push Him over to the side. The pieces just won't fit there."

"It's about time for Mother to quote her favorite verse," said Tom.

So I quoted it: "God, in Christ, reconciling the world unto Himself."

After the students had left, Fred went back to the hospital to check on his heart case. Tom took Vicki outside to see if he could

79

make her see the constellations, so far a losing battle. Judy sat very still in her chair, as I picked up the burfee plates and started for the kitchen.

"Mother, wait a minute," she said. Something had been troubling her ever since she first came from school. "What would you say if . . ." I set the plates back on the table and sat down. "What would you say if I told you I was going to become a Hindu?"

It was a good thing I had sat down. "What did you say, Judy?" I stalled.

"What would you say if I told you I was going to become a Hindu?" She did not take her eyes off my face.

"You're not joking?" I knew she wasn't. Her deep brown eyes could not have been more serious.

"I am not joking," she said.

What was there for me to say? I had said it all so many times that I had thought the question would never arise. That sweet, earnest, devout child before me, flesh of my flesh, a Hindu! I had never thought of her in any way except as a child of Christ. I had failed her, and I had failed God.

And I had failed the other missionaries, and our Indian Christians. How could I face anybody? All this came over me in a flash, and I was the more deeply shamed in the realization that almost my first reaction was one of loss of face.

She let me sit in silence, until the whole impact of what she had said had sunk in. I saw her whole life before me . . . her marriage. . . . Where was Fred? Perhaps he would be able to cope with this.

I must have looked very stricken, for she suddenly said, "I'm sorry, Mother. I just want you to know how Rani's mother will feel. Rani is going to tell her mother, this vacation, that she is going to become a Christian. When I think how close our family has been, it makes me hurt all over."

She sighed, then came over and kissed me goodnight. After she had gone into her room, I sat there thinking. We Scovels had never had to count the cost of being Christian. "It has been too easy for us," I thought.

One of the Muslim junior staff members who had become a Christian, was poisoned by a member of his family when he returned to Pakistan on a visit. He only narrowly escaped with his life.

The college had a rule that no student could change his religion during his medical course. This removed the temptation from any who might be hopeful of standing in well with teachers for that reason. It also gave the serious ones time to consider thoroughly what the step would mean, and the price they would have to pay in severing community and family ties. Yet there were those stalwarts who hazarded everything and were baptized after they graduated.

"How dare we do this to Indian families?" I asked our Indian padri the next time I saw him.

"Many of us have been through it," said Padri Amos Boyd, smiling a little sadly. "It is not easy. But surely you believe that in the end it is worth any sacrifice! And many of us have had the joy of opening the lives of our parents to the love of Christ and of seeing them completely changed by the happiness it has brought them. . . . And remember, it is not *we* who are doing it; it is the Holy Spirit, God Himself who is seeking the lost and the lonely."

Rani's family were far wiser, from their standpoint, than I would have been. "They treated the whole thing as a good joke," Judy wrote, when she got back to school. "They told all their friends, in front of her, the hilarious story of her wanting to become a Christian."

Rani did not become a Christian.

chapter eleven

The children went back to Woodstock in March.

"I don't like it," said Fred the day after they had left. "This house is unbearably neat. No shoes under chairs; my nail scissors are just where I left them; my mucilage is in front of me when I want it; I even have a pencil to use. I don't like it at all."

Our life during the next years revolved around Woodstock School's winter vacation, and our summer holiday. Fred would take me to the hills one weekend in late June. With us would be Chandru, his wife, Umda, and their little son, Sri Chand. Balu would remain behind to keep house for Fred. We would open one of the mission houses which were provided so that families could be with their children during the summer months. We lost no time in taking ours out of boarding.

On one of these precious days before our long separation for the summer, Fred and I would pack a lunch, climb to our favorite spot in the mountains, and gather enough pine cones for our winter fires. We would come back in the late afternoon before the children got home from school, grateful for every moment we had had in that singing silence.

Fred would have to return by Sunday afternoon. We would watch him walk down the mountain, and wait for his wave at the last curve before he disappeared. Later he would come back for his vacation. Then the family would have picnics together, long hikes into the hills, or shopping sprees for Christmas gifts in Mussoorie Bazaar. We always stopped at the sweet shop to buy jelabis. It was fun to watch the hot oil bubbling in the caldron as the pretzel-shaped sweets were dropped in, to see them swell to a golden brown just before they were popped into newspaper cornucopias for eating on the way home.

Except during the short period of Fred's vacation from the stifling heat of the plains, the writing I was doing for the Indian Church kept me occupied all summer. After a year or two at the library, we had been able to get a fine young Indian to take my place. Eric Massey was a trained librarian and did far better at the job than I had done. The Synod next assigned me as Interchurch Correspondent, which meant getting out several articles and news notes each month. This was an interchange of ideas and inspiration, derived from the work of the church in India, and shared with the churches around the world with whom United Presbyterians were related. The writing could be done much better in the quiet of Landour during the hours when the children were in school.

Too, we mothers took turns serving on the P.T.A., or on the Board of Managers of Landour Community Hospital.

Fred came up for Tom's graduation in June of 1956, following which Tom left us to return to America for college at Wooster, Ohio. How does a mother endure that final moment when her child clings to her before he goes out into the world alone?

The summer before had had its special excitement.

"Mother, mother, come he-e-e-ere!" screamed Vicki, one evening as I was taking the usual bird bath in our small tin tub. I grabbed a towel and hurried into the bedroom. Before I got the door open, I had heard the news. "Anne is enga-a-a-aged!" We were all so excited we danced around the room, reading the cablegram which had just been delivered.

As the excitement died down, the miles lengthened between us. On the day we had left America, Anne had burst into tears saying, "Mommy, I just thought of something. I could graduate from nursing school, get married, and have a couple of children before I ever see you again."

I put my hands under the lapels of her old green coat and lifted the collar around her chin. "I can think of something worse, honey," I told her, "that all this *wouldn't* happen to you!" We said goodbye at the hotel elevator before I fled to my room to cry a good share of the night.

Now she had graduated, and now she would be married without the bride's father to take her down the aisle, the bride's mother to weep in the front pew, the bride's sisters to be attendants.

But we were so overjoyed at her joy, and followed the plans with such excitement that again we felt we had been given that peace which does pass any understanding of it. If we had had the whole universe from which to choose, we could not have found a man more perfect for Anne than our new son, John Ashley Fitch, whose grandparents had been missionaries in our part of China.

And we had the same emotions to live through again, and felt exactly the same about our new daughter, Faith Greeley, whom Carl married in the summer of 1958.

"At least our new children can't complain of mother-in-law trouble from this distance," said Fred.

Meanwhile, we had a wedding nearer home which we did attend. I returned from the hills each year as early in September as I could terminate committee meetings and other Landour responsibilities. So I was well started in the Ludhiana routine by October when we left for Delhi for the Garst wedding.

Dr. Ronald Garst, an American Methodist, was an orthopedic surgeon on our staff. Two years previously, he and his family had been driving from Oklahoma to take ship for India. His wife had taken her turn driving; Ron and the two small children had dozed off. Whether or not his wife had fallen asleep at the wheel, Ron never knew. The car was smashed against a tree; his wife had been killed, and he and Linda and David were taken to the hospital.

When the three recovered, they continued with their plans to serve God in India.

"I was too numb to do anything else," Ron told us. We marveled at the way he managed to open the department in the new hospital, set up a shop where artificial limbs were made, and be both mother and father to the two children.

We were delighted when Ron found Marie Mathews, a beautiful young widow who had had her own tragedies. She loved, and was loved by, David and Linda. The wedding in Delhi was pure joy.

The drive back to Ludhiana was anything else but. The Autumn rain was "sluishing" down in an unprecedented pour. We had one hundred and fifty miles to drive along the Grand Trunk Road, lined on either side by trees which had been there before Kipling wrote about Kim's journey on the same thoroughfare. Now many of those trees had fallen in the storm and were lying in the road, blocking our progress. The men would get out, hack through the branches (no veteran in India ever travels without a hatchet), and on we would go for another mile or so.

We were riding with Carl Taylor who was driving his jeep station wagon. He never lost patience for a moment. He simply followed the pattern—drive, stop the car, men out, hack; men in, drive, stop the car, hack. We counted eighty-two trees down in that stretch of road.

By two o'clock in the morning (we had left at seven in the evening), Carl turned off at Ambala, half way between Delhi and Ludhiana. We had David and Linda with us. Carl and his lovely wife, Mary, were going to look after them along with their three, while the newlyweds had a brief honeymoon. Carl thought the two Garst children had had enough for one day. He would drive to the mission compound at Ambala and give them a little sleep before starting out next morning.

"Just drop us off at the railway station," Fred said. "I've got an early class this morning."

We got what proved to be the last train out for several weeks.

We arrived in Ludhiana at about three-thirty that morning. The rain had stopped for a while, but we had had a normal year's supply—twenty-eight inches—during the first twenty-four hours. (It soon began again and continued for two more days and nights, flooding the whole countryside. Carl Taylor and his Preventive Medicine students, girls and boys, did a heroic job of flood relief—all of them wading chest-high across country to take food and medicines and to rescue villagers.)

As our pedicab driver splashed through the puddles on our way from the station, we were amazed to find people clustered in groups at streetcorners, usually completely deserted at this hour.

"That's funny," said Fred. "What's up? I wonder."

"Do you think it could be some special day at the temple? You know how early the women go with their offerings," I suggested.

"No, I don't think so," Fred replied. "These people don't seem to be going anywhere. They look as if they were waiting for something to happen."

For once, our pedicab driver had no explanation to offer.

We were even more amazed, when we reached our compound, to see the lights on in the church, and to find it filled with people praying.

Sudhir Roy, our executive secretary, was just coming out of the church, his long black overcoat almost covering his white pajamas.

"These people! I can't do anything with them," he said in answer to Fred's question. "They think the end of the world is coming."

"Where did they ever get that idea?" asked Fred.

"The rumor got started through a radio broadcast early in the evening," Mr. Roy replied. "Someone has predicted a terrible earthquake which will bury us all. I've told our dear church people that no seismograph predicts an earthquake; it simply records it when it happens. I would surely like to know how that rumor got started." He hunched himself down into his coat to keep warm.

"What time is it due?" I asked.

"Four o'clock," replied Mr. Roy.

Fred looked at his watch. "Whew, that doesn't give us much time. Come on, honey, if the end of the world is coming, I've got to have a cup of coffee."

"You two!" smiled Mr. Roy, shaking his head slowly. "I'd better stay here until the hour passes." He went back into the church.

When we opened the front door, the house smelled dank and musty. I went at once to the kitchen to make the coffee.

"Fred, I can't get this door open," I called. It took all his strength to push the door open enough for us to see in. The mud roof had collapsed, completely burying the kitchen. I began to feel that the end of the world might as well come. But we found an enamel pitcher, some powdered coffee, and an immersion heater in the dining-room cupboard, and we had our coffee. The world remained in orbit.

We heard later that a gang of thieves had started the rumor to get everyone out of their houses. Their ruse worked, we were told; they made quite a haul in the city that night.

chapter twelve

It was while working at Mr. Roy's house that I had another near encounter with a reptile, this time with only the ghost of a snake.

The historical records of the mission were kept in a cement vault under the executive secretary's house. I had been asked to do some sorting and clearing out, and had been spending an hour or two each day in the vault. One afternoon, Mr. Roy came over to our house to tell me he had found a cobra skin three feet long on the steps leading from the records room. The snake had evidently been inside for some time. It had slithered under the door and had shed its skin on the steps.

My face must have turned white as I dropped into the nearest chair, too weak in the knees to stand.

"You're not looking very well," said Mr. Roy, inching his

heavy frame forward in the narrow rocker. "You need to get out of that vault for a while and take a day in the country. When are we going to visit the village of Sadhu Sundar Singh? We've talked about it so long. Let's make a date right now."

I had read about Sadhu Sundar Singh before coming to India. This Christian had donned the traditional saffron robes of a holy man, and had walked the roads of India, telling his people the good news of Christ's coming. I had been collecting stories of the Sadhu from those who had known him, or who had been told of him by their parents. Mr. Roy had promised to take me to Rampur, the village where Sundar Singh had been born.

"I'll go any time you are free to take me," I said.

"Then let's make it Monday next," said Mr. Roy. "Shall we say about one o'clock? I'll get a driver for the station wagon." I forgot all about the snake.

We had to shout our goodbyes at the door. Crows, hundreds of them, were coming in from the day's foraging. Jostling each other, they filled the trees in the compound in their usual raucous settling down for the night. I didn't know whether to be crude and offer Mr. Roy an umbrella to get home, or to just let him take his chances. I decided in favor of the latter.

Mr. Roy's offering to take time out from his busy schedule to take me to Rampur was typical of the many thoughtful ways he found to make us feel at home in India, and a part of the life of the Indian Church. This man was not only an executive; he was a much-beloved pastor, an agricultural expert, and an educator. His work as principal of the Moga Training School for Village Teachers was unique. In addition to completing the work for a primary-school teaching certificate, Mr. Roy's students had to be able to grow cotton, spin it, weave it, and make it into a garment; shelter, raise, and feed animals; grow a garden for food, including raising wheat to make into flat breads called *chapatis;* tan leather and make their own shoes; raise silkworms. In short, they had to know how to live successfully as members of the village community in which they would be teaching.

Mr. Roy himself was not afraid to work with his hands, and though it was revolutionary to see a man in his position doing menial tasks, the students learned to love and respect him for it.

One story they liked to tell was of the day Mr. Roy was at the top of a ladder whitewashing a wall. A terrible flood had devastated the school, and Mr. Roy was getting the buildings into shape again. A government Inspector of Schools arrived and demanded to see the principal. "Just a moment," said Mr. Roy, and finished his brush stroke across the wall.

"You rascal! Get down off that ladder and call your principal," said the inspector.

Mr. Roy slowly descended the ladder and turned to face the man. "I am the principal," he said to the amazed inspector.

So that I could be free to go to Rampur on Monday, Fred took my language study hour with our new teacher, Mr. Bhagat Singh, a young Sikh gentleman, a Punjabi. He was an excellent teacher, and besides our language study, gave us much of the culture and tradition of the Punjab. We had had to lose Daisy and Taj when we stopped full-time language study. They had been assigned to take on the Hunters, a new young couple, who had come out to do art work for Christian publications.

Monday turned out to be one of those perfect autumn days when the sky was as blue as a pottery bowl, and the world was flecked with sunlight. As we headed for Rampur, I could hardly believe that I was on the way to the village of Sadhu Sundar Singh. During our drive, Mr. Roy told me more about him.

"His mother must have been a remarkable woman," said Mr. Roy. "You know they were a devout Sikh family. She had her son taught, not only their own Sikh holy book, the Granth, but, do you know, that child knew the whole of the Hindu Bhagavad

Gita by heart when he was only five years old? He read the Koran, and some of the Upanishads, too.

"Sundar Singh had no patience with people who commiserated with him over his mother's not being able to be with him in heaven because she was not a Christian. He would say, 'My mother prepared me for the work of God, and the Holy Spirit made me a Christian. Whenever I think of her, I thank God for such a mother; she had a wonderful amount of light.' "

"What was his father like?" I asked.

"His father was a good man," said Mr. Roy, "but he didn't understand his son. How could he? One minute the boy was burning Bibles in the village square because he hated all Christians—his father was horrified at anyone burning a holy book; the next minute, the lad was telling his father he had become a Christian. This shocked his father even more. He didn't know what to do with him. Someone suggested he be sent to Ludhiana to school. You know he studied in the very building which will be your new outpatient department in the hospital.

"There was turmoil in Sadhu Sundar Singh's heart until he had his vision," Mr. Roy went on. He had brought along Bishop A. J. Appasamy's biography, *Sundar Singh*. "Let me read you what Sundar Singh himself says about his vision. Here it is." Mr. Roy had been flipping pages as he spoke.

"'Though I thought I had done a good deed in burning the Gospel, yet my unrest of heart increased. On the third day, when I felt I could bear it no longer, I got up at three in the morning and, after bathing, prayed that if there was a God at all He would reveal himself to me, and show me the way of salvation. I firmly made up my mind that if this prayer was not answered, I would before daylight go down to the railway, and place my head on the line before the incoming train.

"'I remained till about half past four, praying and waiting and expecting to see Krishna or Buddha, or some other avatar of the Hindu religion; they appeared not, but a light was shining in the room. I opened the door to see where it came from, but all was dark outside. I returned inside, and the light increased in intensity and took the form of a globe of light above the ground, and in this light there appeared, not the form I had expected, but the living Christ whom I had counted as dead. To all eternity I shall never forget His glorious loving face, nor the few words which He spoke: "Why do you persecute me? See, I have died on the cross for you and for the whole world." These words were burned into my heart as by lightning, and I fell to the ground before Him. My heart was filled with inexpressible joy and peace, and my whole life was entirely changed.' "

So changed was his life that after he was expelled from the shelter of his wealthy, cultured home, he walked the roads of India and on into Tibet without money and with only the food given him along the way. After his journeys for God had taken him around the world to stand before kings, he set out once more for Tibet on an April day in 1929. He disappeared, never to be heard of again.

"Do you think we will be able to find his family?" asked our driver as we crossed the little bridge leading into Rampur village. "It's been a long time, and his family had disowned him, hadn't they?"

"Yes, but he visited his village occasionally," said Mr. Roy.

We stopped the car in one of the narrow streets, and stepped out. Mr. Roy made inquiries in Punjabi.

"Of course the house is known to us," said an old Sikh patriarch with a long white beard. "No one who ever truly worships God can remain hidden."

We walked down the dark maze of narrow streets where Sundar Singh had played, avoiding one of the goats whose ancestor had probably followed the thoughtful little boy with the faraway look in his eyes. At the carved stone arch of an old doorway, we were welcomed by a very happy group of rela-

95

tives. One of the village children had evidently run ahead to warn the family of our arrival.

The house had seen better days. We climbed the rickety wooden stairs to a cool room on the roof, stepping around cotton which was spread out to dry. We were ushered into the room, and seated upon woven string beds covered with embroidered shawls. Most of the relatives were women, but a handsome young black-bearded grand-nephew of Sundar Singh acted as host. The other men were working in a field some distance from the village, we were told.

"What do you remember about Sundar Singh?" Mr. Roy asked one old woman.

"I remember that he told us all about the countries of the world," she said, "and that he wore the yellow homespun of a sadhu, and that his face was young and very beautiful."

"He was very simple in his habits and ate only the commonest food," remembered another.

"There was no one in the whole village to compare with him," said the oldest woman present. "Will we ever see him again?"

Mr. Roy told the family in a very simple way that it was our Christian hope and belief that we would see him again, and that such was also the belief of their brother, Sundar Singh.

"This boy is our religious one," said the same old lady, pointing to the grandnephew.

"Your home should be the light of the whole village," Mr. Roy said to him.

"Did you know him?" the young man asked.

"Yes, I remember him very well," said Mr. Roy. "At one time, he lived in a tent in back of our home at the Saharanpur Theological Seminary. My father was principal then, and I was a young student at the seminary.

"Once Sundar Singh told me a story. He said that he was walking along the road to Tibet. He was hungry and he had no money. He stopped at a house by the side of the road and asked for a drink. 'What is your name?' the woman asked. 'Sundar Singh', he replied. 'I have a parcel here for you; it has been waiting for some time,' the woman said. It turned out to be a Christmas cake sent to him by a friend in England. Inside the cake were two sovereigns—enough to take him the rest of his journey.

It was time to go. We had drunk our tea, and we had been to the fields to visit the older men who all came with us to the jeep. Mr. Roy turned to the young grandnephew. "Do you have a Bible?" he asked.

"Yes," replied the young man, smiling, "I have the Bible in Punjabi, Urdu, Hindi, and English."

I could hardly wait to get home to tell Fred about our wonderful day.

chapter thirteen

I wished so much that Fred could have been with me on the trip to Sundar Singh's village. He would have enjoyed every minute of it. But the constant influx of patients and the heavy teaching schedule kept him close to the hospital. For the first time in our married life, our work was taking us along separate paths. I was not sure that I liked the idea. Telling him about it afterward was not like sharing an experience with him.

But I enjoyed the writing, and that was what I had been assigned to do; I knew I was needed in this field more than as another nurse at the hospital.

Now I was off on another village trip—this time to gather material to write up Padri Fazl-ud-Din's Economic Uplift Program. Padri Sahib was the director and the moving spirit behind the program. He was also the most energetic Indian we knew.

The story we were told of his younger days as a pastor was characteristic of him.

He had been preaching in a village courtyard to a group of low-caste Punjabis (Gandhi called them *Harijans*—"Children of God.") The pastor's talk was interrupted by a Hindu lawyer who said, "Pay no attention to what this Christian is telling you. We are the ones who provide for you and who really care about you."

Padri Fazl-ud-Din was not known for his patience. He strode down the aisle, took the lawyer by the collar, and led him out of the village to the only well from which untouchables were allowed to draw water.

"You really care about these people, do you?" he asked. "Then show them that you care by taking one cup of water from their well." The lawyer ran away as fast as he could.

Today this pastor was taking me to see some of the people who had received loans from the Economic Uplift Program.

"You see," Padri Sahib was explaining, "we have to raise the standard of living of village Christians if the church is to help itself; and more important, if it is to reach out to help others."

As we walked down the narrow village street with the dirty drain in the center unable to cope with the refuse; as we saw the dilapidated thatched roofs of unrepaired mud houses, a few listless people standing in doorways, it was not difficult to understand what he meant.

"But how does it work?" I asked.

"I will show you," he replied.

We stopped at a home down the street. One of the children ushered us into a neat little courtyard where his mother was sitting on the floor of the veranda running a sewing machine. She got up as we came in. I was introduced to Mrs. Bali and was told her story.

The Bali family had lost everything at the time of the partitioning of India into India and Pakistan. Wandering homeless and lost, they had come to the town of Hoshiarpur. Here Mr. Bali met the venerable missionary, the Rev. Joseph Barrows. After many talks with him and with other Christians in the town, Mr. and Mrs. Bali and the children were baptized. Mr. Bali became a teacher. But his small salary provided barely enough to feed the family.

"And there were all the other things we needed," said Mrs. Bali, throwing the chiffon scarf of her Punjabi suit back across her shoulder, as if to rid herself of those memories by the gesture. "Why, clothes for the five of us were costing fifteen rupees a month. Of course, the tailor got most of it."

(All Punjabi families, however poor, patronize the tailor, I learned.)

"Then one day I thought, If I only had a sewing machine, I could do that sewing myself." She beamed at Padri Fazl-ud-Din. "So Padri Sahib helped us."

"We loaned her two hundred thirty rupees to buy the sewing machine," said Padri Sahib. "Now she is sewing for her family and for others in the school compound. She is taking in about the same amount she used to give the tailor. Already she has paid us half the amount she owes us for the machine."

We admired Mrs. Bali's handiwork, drank tall glasses of sweetened tea, and said goodbye. "I don't envy you your job," I told Padri Sahib. "It must be very difficult to collect from these poor villagers."

Padri Sahib was leading me across the fields to see an old widow. I was having a hard time keeping up with this vigorous, wiry man ahead of me. We had to balance ourselves on the narrow foot-high ridges separating the fields. His agility amazed me; he threw back answers to my questions without even looking to see where he was going.

"On the contrary, I have no trouble at all," said Padri Sahib. "We've been going a year, and to date, four hundred and forty-nine Christians have been helped by loans. Almost one hundred per cent have paid back something. And I haven't given up on those other three fellows, either. Take the sewing machines—we've bought twenty-seven of them. Most folks pay back ten to twenty rupees a month until the machine is paid for."

I stopped asking questions until we were back in the jeep. I didn't want to miss a word.

"But are all Punjabis so full of integrity?" I asked.

Padri Sahib smiled a wry smile. "Oh no. You see, we make the elders of the local church responsible for recommending people. Then they have to collect if anyone is negligent in his payments. The elders choose carefully; there *are* many good, deserving people.

"Take these widows for example," Padri Sahib went on. "You have no idea of the plight of these women. They are a drain on an already impoverished family. They have to live on two or three annas a day—not enough for one good meal. The active young people who can work in the fields must be fed first, or the family will not survive at all. We've loaned money for sewing machines to ten or twelve of these widows."

We had stopped at a doorway. "Here's old Mrs. Mohan Masih. She now earns about three rupees a day—more than twenty times what she used to have to eke out her existence."

Because of the strange foreign visitor, the gnarled little woman was shy at first. But her enthusiasm over her new-found economic freedom, and her gratitude to Padri Fazl-ud-Din, soon made her voluble. The more she talked, the more her eyes sparkled with happiness. When Padri Sahib told her that I was from the Church in America which had given the money for her loan, she wanted to prepare a meal for us. It was difficult to tear ourselves away. We wanted to get to Moga before sundown.

"You must meet young Rahamat Masih," explained Padri Sahib. On the way he told me his story.

Rahamat Masih had been a truck mechanic. He had accompanied a Sikh motor driver in that capacity when his truck had been hired to take a wedding party to a village for the usual festivities. The truck was in bad shape, and after the drinks served at the party, the driver was in an even worse condition. There was a crash, darkness, and when Rahamat Masih woke up, he found himself in our hospital at Ludhiana, his leg almost hopelessly crushed. For a time it looked as if Rahamat would be a cripple for the rest of his life. He was a very bitter, very depressed young man.

A Canadian surgeon on the staff, Dr. William Virgin, had taken time to sit down by Rahamat's bed to talk to him about his soul. The hospital evangelist had urged him to give his life completely to Christ—broken leg, shattered hopes, and all. The day came when Rahamat was able to walk out of the hospital and face the world.

"He went to live with his brother who was teaching at the Moga Training School for Village Teachers," said Padri Sahib. "That's where I met him. Together we decided that Rahamat should start a tea stall where the boys from the school could come for snacks."

This was the place Padri Sahib wanted me to see. Rahamat Masih welcomed us with a quiet smile, his large brown eyes appraising me. Padri Sahib introduced us, and told why we had come. Rahamat was not at all sure he wanted to be written up; his uncertainty was clearly visible in his face. Padri Fazl-ud-Din explained that it was for the encouragement of other Christians around the world. Satisfied, Rahamat showed us the counters he had made himself; the stove, the utensils, everything bought with his twenty-dollar loan, now entirely repaid.

At one end of the shop he had set up a display of Christian literature.

"The boys kid me about it," he said, softly, "but they do buy it, and they read it."

"He is a fine young man," said Padri Sahib, as we drove away. Our route lay toward home. Across the Punjab plain, the rose of sunset was coloring the irrigation ditches, brushing the plumes of secundra grass, and dyeing the farmers' faces a deeper tan.

Fred and I never ceased to marvel at what India had been able to accomplish in the brief decade of her independence. The excellent roads left by the British were kept in good repair; irrigation ditches were continually appearing, their gold-colored soil piling up in new places; farmers were more and more riding tractors home from the fields, though we passed a few teams of plodding, cream-white bullocks. Seeing the noble faces of those animals, I could never be surprised that Hindus held them in reverence.

We did not stop again, but Padri Sahib pointed out the villages where his people lived, and told me the stories as we sped along.

I learned about Dula, the flute player of Jagraon, who had saved sixty rupees toward buying a flute of his own.

"The old man always had to rent one when he played at weddings, so he didn't make much profit," Padri Sahib explained. "He had worked hard over the years to save that much.

You know, he became obsessed with the fear that he'd lose the money. He kept changing the hiding place. One day he came to me and asked what he should do. He couldn't sleep nights, worrying about thieves."

"Give me your sixty rupees," Padri Sahib told him. "I will loan you forty more, and we will buy your flute. Then as you earn money, you can repay me."

Dula became a new man.

Across the fields was the house of Bahadur, son of Tara. He had been pulled out of school when he was twelve years old to help support the family. They had lost everything in a recent flood, and had been loaned money for a new beginning.

I heard about Bhajno, a young widow with three small children.

"What do you think you can do to help yourself and your children?" Padri Sahib had asked her.

"Well, if I had a flock of goats . . . but goats cost too much money. I would be afraid of such a big loan. Suppose that something should happen to me," she replied.

"You might start in a small way," Padri Sahib suggested. "If you bought a few small kids, they would only cost two or three rupees each. You could raise them carefully and in time you would have a flock."

"I used to be good with young animals, and I'd like to try," Bhajno had told her pastor.

"She has paid back sixty of the hundred rupees we loaned her, and is now giving regularly to her church," said Padri Fazl-ud-Din. "She is very proud of her church. Praying Hyde himself baptized the first Christians in the village. She *should* be proud. That little church, without even a building in which to meet, is giving regularly to Home Missions, to the Bible Society, toward a scholarship for Baring Christian College, to the Theological Seminary at Saharanpur. They are even giving toward the support of the Dyalls."

"The Dyalls?" I asked.

"Surely you know the Din Dyalls, our foreign missionaries in Africa," said Padri Sahib.

"Oh yes," I replied, and let it go at that. I couldn't explain that it never occurred to me that a church with no building of its own would be helping to support a foreign missionary.

Padri Sahib was still telling me about his people when we came into our compound.

Fred was at the door to meet us when we arrived. He expressed his disappointment to Padri Fazl-ud-Din at not being able to accept his invitation to make the rounds of the parishioners with us.

"Judging from the looks of you, you've both had a wonderful day," said Fred.

"We have," I assured him. "I can't wait to tell you all about it."

Padri Fazl-ud-Din declined the cup of coffee and the few moments of rest we suggested.

"I must get back," he said. "But you must both come with me next time."

"I thought you'd never get here," said Fred as Padri Sahib drove away. "I've had enough of this going our own separate ways. I've decided to take you with me to Vellore."

chapter fourteen

"I couldn't possibly go with you to Vellore," I told my unrealistic husband. "I've got too much to do."

"If you're at the point where you think you're indispensable, you've got to go with me," he replied.

He was to attend the annual fall Council meeting of our sister medical college in South India. From the time of our arrival in India, we had talked of seeing the hospitals and teaching set-ups in Vellore and at the Miraj Medical Centre in western India. The logical time to do it was when Fred represented Ludhiana at the Council meeting. There always seemed to be good reasons why I shouldn't go with him. This time he overruled them all.

"The children are in school; Mildred will postpone the Christmas music for a week; and you can do your writing on the way. You may even get some new ideas."

Just as the train was leaving the Ludhiana station, an Indian gentleman jumped into the compartment with us.

"Dusty traveling these days, isn't it?" he began.

That is all it took to begin a conversation through which we learned that, one, he was a sculptor who had spent three years in a Greenwich Village (New York) apartment; two, he had apparently become one of the foremost sculptors in India today; three, he was engaged in a program to revive village art, under the Indian government's Five-Year-Plan; four, that he was on his way back to Delhi after visiting one of his village projects.

"India may be one of the few countries left in the world where it is not too late to keep its indigenous art from being stifled by industrialization," he said.

"A creative approach such as yours could set a pattern for the rest of us," said Fred.

The sculptor told us how his team had gone into a village, had given out paints for a mural contest, the only instructions being that the painting should be done on the interior walls of the villagers' homes. Overnight, the whole appearance of the village had changed. The painting on the wall had inspired the villager to mend his hearth, replaster the floor, and clean out the drains around his dwelling. The women of the house had polished the brass and had arranged the utensils on newly cleaned shelves. Nobody had suggested that the country people do this; a new self-respect had been released through their creativity.

"Here is my card. I do hope you will visit my studio before too long," said our companion as the train slid into the Delhi station.

"I'm glad you made me come," I told Fred as our sculptor

waved goodbye. "I'd forgotten how interesting the outside world could be."

"Mugazzeen! Mugazeen!" a hawker cried. It had been a long, long time since I had purchased a magazine at a railway station. I chose "a leading American woman's magazine." As the train moved out into the country, Fred settled down with the contents of his brief case in preparation for the coming meetings, while I turned the thick, sleek pages of another world.

"Clothes for Summer Travel" caught my eye. Pictured were the compact little suitcases designed to hold enough clothes for two weeks, delectable clothes—navy blue with white accessories, a glittering sheath for evening. Nowhere did I see an unwieldy bedding roll, a water jug of red clay stuck into a wooden frame, or a tiffin basket for carrying food. There was no plastic bag containing toilet paper, soap, towels, and newspaper for wiping off cinders before sitting down.

I looked down at my travel costume—full Punjabi trousers of silk, a long tunic of flowered blue. Around my shoulders from front to back was the blue chiffon scarf which could be thrown over my head to avoid cinders, or tie up a sack of sweets, or wipe a running nose. I used it only to avoid cinders, but I had seen this *chuni* used in as many ways as George Washington Carver had used peanuts.

Before dark we passed a flooded area where trees, chest-deep in water, were raising frantic arms for help as we sped by. The darkness closed us in. Miraculously we were alone in our third-class coach.

"Time for my exercise," said Fred. He began to unfold the air mattresses we had borrowed from Don and Rusty Rice. Don Rice had come to Ludhiana as a representative of the Disciples of Christ, to take Carl Taylor's place after Carl had been called to Harvard's School of Public Health, where he was to put on a special course for doctors from overseas using the plan for teaching Preventive Medicine he had used for our students.

Don Rice was tall, not given to many words, but in his quiet way he continued to build up the Department of Preventive Medicine in Ludhiana. Rusty, his auburn-haired wife, was my steam valve. She always knew just when to suggest a cup of coffee and her special Russian tea cakes.

The night before we left for Vellore, Don and Rusty had come over to the house with the air mattresses. We were to bless them for it later.

"Those boards can really get hard," said Don. "You'd better take these along."

Now I watched Fred's cheeks puff out and his face turn red as he blew them up.

"Just imagine sleeping on your husband's breath," I said.

The train rocketed through the night as we slept.

Throughout the next day, the landscape gradually changed character. By evening the train window became a watercolor—chartreuse rice fields with white birds above them, the full red-and-gold skirt of a young bride following her husband across the fields, a blue-painted trunk on her head.

The city reached fingers into the countryside.

"Here we are at Madras," said Fred.

As we walked through the modern station building, there was just a whiff in the air of Grand Central Station—that combination of time table print, chocolate candy wrappers, stale train smoke, and people. Fred went ahead to buy the tickets for Katpadi, where the Vellore jeep would pick us up.

Dr. Ida Scudder and Vellore Christian Medical College! We had heard about them and read about them for years. Now we were

seeing them both in person. (The institution had a very living personality of its own, only part of it acquired from this radiant lady.) Dr. Ida entertained us at dinner. Her white hair framed a dynamic face, for all her eighty-some years. Listening to her and seeing her interest and encouragement in what we were doing made us want to go out into the world and "lick our weight in wildcats." What vision that woman had!

Sitting beside Dr. Ida was an outstanding Indian colleague, Dr. Hilda Lazarus. Dr. Lazarus was small, black-haired, wiry—as animated as Dr. Ida was serene. She had retired as Director of the Medical College, but had come back for the Council meeting. It was Dr. Lazarus who showed us around the college, its solid, graystone buildings softened by a lily pool or a bank of flowering shrubs.

The day before Council meeting, I went with Fred the four miles from the college to the hospital in the city. Fred saw "everyone-and-his-second-cousin" who had anything to do with the institution. Armed with notebook and pencil, and a battery of questions, he went from office to office, firing away a full barrage. As I was on hand to serve coffee, I noted that the Vellore staff came up smiling, even as the onslaught continued through every break in Council meeting the following day.

The meetings over, we left the same night for Bangalore where we would change trains for Miraj.

As we traveled across the tip of India, and then north, the scene changed again. The chopped-top palm trees gave place to grove after grove of coconut trees whose huge fronds seemed carelessly pinned to the trunks by a few coconuts, like a child's paper pinwheel on the end of a pencil. It seemed that everyone was either wearing flowers or selling them; women's "buns" at the back of their heads were completely covered with flowers to match their saris. Children wore elaborate headdresses of them. To add to the gaiety, the landmarkers along the railway were painted vermilion instead of the usual white.

By noon we were steadily climbing, and at the top of a steep grade, we were delayed several hours. From a tiny village in the distance, three or four women came running across the fields with baskets on their heads. The baskets held toys carved from soapstone—all the things which the smallest housekeepers might need: a stove, a grinding mill, trays of "pretend" food, a receptacle for storing grain, buckets and dishes of all kinds. Though our daughters had long since outgrown such toys, I could not resist buying a set. I was ashamed to pay but forty cents when I thought of all the work that had gone into carving them.

We moved on a few miles and stopped again. After what seemed an endless wait, we learned that a freight train had been wrecked somewhere this side of the next station. We would have to walk around the wreck to a train waiting for us on the other side of it.

As we were collecting our belongings for the move, a fine-looking young Indian, barefooted and wearing dirty jeans, came to the door of the compartment and said, in English, "May I help you?"

Jeans! There was only one country in the world which produced them.

"Have you ever been to America?" I asked. "I notice you are wearing American trousers, and your English sounds American."

"Yes," the boy replied. "I represented India on the 4-H Youth Farm Exchange program in your country last year."

We couldn't talk fast enough. He walked with us to the train and sat with us as long as he could. We were, he said, sent from heaven. How else could the wreck have set us down right in the middle of his hundred-acre coconut farm? He had been so lonely without his "families," as he called them. He had lived in three different homes in the state of Washington, and had then gone east to Lancaster, Pennsylvania, where he had lived with three Amish families, a month in turn.

"One of the farmers was an Amish priest. I learned a lot about what he believed," he said, reverently.

One could sense his deep affection for these Americans who had made him feel as if he belonged to them. He spoke of what wonderful cooks the women were.

"But what I really get hungry for is a bowl of canned mushroom soup," he added.

(And so did I; oh, so did I!)

Fred was asking his usual questions. He learned that it takes eight months after planting a coconut tree for it to bear fruit, and that it will produce a maximum yield for about eight years. Harvesting took place once a day for ten months, and about two hundred rupees could be obtained for eleven hundred coconuts. (I gathered that eleven hundred coconuts could be picked up easily almost any morning!) This young farmer, unlike any of his neighbors, also grew cotton, rice, and sugar cane.

"And I'm going to try strawberries," he added. "Soon I am to be the host of an American boy who will come to India as I went there," he said.

What will an American boy think of this hundred-acre coconut farm on a quiet hilltop miles from a movie or a Coke, I wondered.

The train was pulling out. He waved goodbye. It was a reluctant farewell for all three of us. He soon became a dot on the horizon.

We had two days in Miraj, where Fred filled up more notebooks and I enjoyed the paintings of two of the missionaries, Mrs. Ruth Donaldson and Dr. Eugene Evans.

A day in Bombay for business at the Inter-Mission Business Office, a reunion with the Harry Shaws, and we were ready for the last lap of our journey—Bombay to Ludhiana.

Just before the train pulled out of the Bombay Station, I noticed a Muslim kneeling on a square handkerchief spread out on the platform, praying toward Mecca. That Mecca happened to be in the direction of a glass case displaying stainless-steel tumblers, sterilizing bowls, and emesis basins, bothered him not at all. The man's devout face was a study. I prayed, too, that God would answer his prayer in a special way.

We arrived in Ludhiana the next morning.

"It's good to be home," said Fred. "Haven't we had a wonderful time? I'll change into my hospital clothes while Chandru is putting on the breakfast."

"Breakfast is on the table and your coffee is poured," I pleaded.

"It won't take a minute," said my husband. Fred was back in his whirlpool again.

"Yes, we've had a wonderful time," I said to his back as he went upstairs to change.

chapter fifteen

By March of 1957, one set of problems was all tied up in a bundle and filed away. The first section of the new hospital was built. Ron Garst was in charge of moving equipment and patients to the new building. But before that we were to have the official opening.

A huge tent of many brilliant colors had been set up on the hospital grounds. People poured into the compound, the women in their best saris—heavy satins, soft chiffons, encrusted brocades, in every color on a painter's pallet. Children's bright turbans bobbed in and out of the crowd.

At noon, the academic procession formed outside the new hospital. Among the black-and-scarlet gowned, none was as handsome as my husband. I got a lump in my throat I was so proud every time I looked at him.

A car drove in through the front gate, and the Health Minister of all India, Raj Kumari Amrit Kaur, alighted. She was followed by Dr. Eileen Snow, and the two were greeted by each member of the staff.

This great Christian stateswoman was to give the main address. The only other person I have known with her same quiet magnetism was the poet, Leonora Speyer. There was something regal about them both. I had come to know and admire Raj Kumari Amrit Kaur on one of her previous visits to Ludhiana. Dr. Snow had asked me to accompany her throughout the day, to keep her informed of her engagements, and to arrange for her wants. We went from public appearance to public appearance. At one point I said to her, "How do you keep up this pace? After your departure tonight, we will collapse in a heap, but you will get up tomorrow morning and do this all over again in some other city."

She smiled. "I couldn't do it without the strength which comes from prayer," she said.

Now she stood on a dais in the open air with Dr. Snow on her right, and on her left Dean Lakshmi Rao in black gown and white sari bordered with scarlet and gold. The medical students, in white, marched past, eyes right, then formed a guard of honor down which the three women walked through the crowds to the platform inside the tent. Everyone stood as the college orchestra struck up the national anthem.

We were proud to have the assembled multitude hear Eileen Snow's report—thirty-one doctors to graduate, fifteen nurses, twenty-six midwives, seven health visitors, and five laboratory technicians. And we were even more proud when she announced that the man and woman standing highest in the Punjab University's medical examinations were two of our own students.

Then Raj Kumari Amrit Kaur spoke; there was not a cough or a silken rustle among those fifteen hundred people. She told again of the need for trained medical personnel in India. She spoke with gratitude for what our college and hospital had done in the past, and of her dreams for the future health of the people of her country. Then she spoke of the new building.

"It is the spirit which matters most," she said, "not the bricks and mortar, but the spirit of love through which this institution came into being."

After the ribbon across the entrance had been cut, the crowds milled through the hospital. Some of the guests were important people in India's national life—educators, industrialists, well-known medical people who had come from great distances. One of these doctors said, "I haven't seen a hospital like this since I left Zurich, Switzerland."

Fred and I wondered what the Punjabi farmers would think of this modern building, so different from their village homes. Would they be so overawed that they would not want to come to us when they were ill? We needn't have worried. The Punjabi villager is not easily overawed. They accepted the hospital as if it had always been theirs. The only evidence that this was something new and rather wonderful came when the first elevator load went up. Then a lusty cheer arose from those watching. This was the first elevator in Ludhiana.

The day stands out as one of joy and fulfillment. So very much had been accomplished. The building was not yet finished, but three hundred and fifty patients would be moving in within the week. Two pictures of that day remain as special memories— Eileen Snow bending over pansies arranged in a deep plate of Delhi blue pottery, a gift to her from the architect who planned the hospital; and a little Punjabi girl wandering happily through the halls, a live brown chicken under one arm.

"Well, that's that," said Fred, grinning as he flung off his gold-and-green hood and unhooked his gown. "I feel as if I had come to the end of an era. Now all we have to do is to find enough money to keep the place going." His grin faded.

How many man-hours Fred had spent in worry over how to make ends meet during his years in China and India! And as the world counts money, how little it would take to remove all financial burden. Everyone tried so desperately to "make do." I longed to wave a magic wand over this shining new building— to fill the coffers with enough gold, so that not one person who ever worked in it would be hampered by lack of maintenance funds.

But I remembered what Raj Kumari-ji had said three years to the very day before this. She had come to Ludhiana to lay the cornerstone for the building we had just opened. Then we were facing a bigger question: Would there be enough money to build the hospital? Said Raj Kumari that day, "Gandhi-ji once encouraged me by saying, 'No good work languishes because of lack of funds. It languishes only from lack of good workers.' "

One of those good workers was my close friend, Myrtle Cray, who dropped in for a cup of coffee after the celebration.

Myrtle and Raymond Cray had come to India from Ohio State University where Raymond was a member of the faculty. He was in India under the Technical Co-operation Mission of the United States government, and had been assigned to the Indian government's Agricultural College across the city from us.

We two women had our writing in common. Living among scientific people, as we both were, we leaned rather heavily upon each other for literary sustenance. The extra-curricular activities of the Crays included an intense interest in the Ludhiana church and hospital. Myrtle was always looking for something to do for us—"something big!" Once she organized a Hospital Day throughout the city. She got the co-operation of all religious and secular groups. (Who could resist her large eyes, trim figure, beautifully coifed white hair, and quiet smile?) She organized medical exhibits which would interest the laity. Visitors could have their blood pressure taken, see X-rays of their insides, watch a cast being applied, and take part in first-aid demonstrations. Exhibits were set up by the Department of Preventive Medicine on how to make smokeless village stoves and bore-hole latrines. Myrtle arranged a luncheon for the V.I.P.s, and altogether succeeded in raising a sizable amount for the charity work of the hospital.

The next of the Crays' projects was to interest their Community Church in Columbus, Ohio, in buying and shipping out an electrocardiograph, an instrument which was an invaluable asset to Fred in his heart-specialty work.

"I wish everyone who's read *The Ugly American* could meet you two," I said to her after that book came out.

chapter sixteen

Then, as had happened so many times before in our years as missionaries, the whole pattern of our life suddenly changed.

I was in Landour when the letter came. The mailman had come around the corner of the veranda as Ernestine Sauer and I were having our morning coffee break. We were close enough friends to take our individual letters from husband or children and read them to ourselves as we drank our coffee, reading aloud portions each knew would interest the other. I paid so little attention to one sentence in my daily letter from Fred, that I almost neglected to read it out:

"Doug Forman wants me to take his job in New York when he retires as Secretary of the Christian Medical Council for Overseas Work.'"

"Will he take it?" asked Ernestine.

"I can't imagine it," I said, and dismissed the idea.

Fred's letter later in the week commented, "You didn't react to your husband's new job prospect. What do you think of being the wife of a desk man? Ugh!"

I didn't know what to think. We talked it over when he came up to the hills for his vacation. We went up into the mountains, and sat down to look at the distant snows.

"Heaven knows, the last thing I want to do is to sit behind a desk," said Fred. "But even before this letter came, I'd been questioning in my mind whether or not we should come back to Ludhiana after our furlough. I've been thinking a lot about the children lately, and our responsibility to them. I just don't know whether or not its right to leave them alone in America for six years as we have the others. Judy and Vicki have had a sheltered life here; I'd hate to throw them into life in America today with no parents on hand when they needed them. I'm not getting any younger, either. If I'm going to enjoy my children, I'd better get started doing it."

"You haven't said a word about this," I told him.

"I didn't want to upset you. I know how much you've missed them. Anyway, nothing was settled in my mind. It isn't now," he replied. He thought a moment before going on.

"I told you after the hospital opening that I felt as if I had come to the end of an era. I'm feeling it more and more. I was sent out to help with the upgrading, and with the building of the new hospital. Both jobs are finished. We're recognized as an M.B.B.S. degree-giving medical college; the pioneers will graduate before we leave in fifty-nine; the new bylaws are almost ready to be passed; the World Health Organization nomenclature is complete and up to date. Zelma Virgin is doing a whale of a job in the new record room; the doctors can find any chart they want in a matter of minutes. Somehow I feel as if I'd done what I was sent here to do."

"What about your medical department?" I asked. He had been

sitting forward, intense with thinking aloud. Now he dropped back against the hill and squinted at the sky.

"With a staff like ours, anyone can take my place," he answered. "It isn't like being the only doctor in an area of five million people, as it was in China."

I, too, lay back on the ground and looked up at the sky. The sun broke through a cloud at the moment a thought really came home to me—we wouldn't have to leave Judy and Vicki alone in America! We wouldn't have to leave all six of them after our furlough. Why, we might even get completely unpacked and have a home of our own! I began to talk to him about my dream house.

"Will you carry your bride over your own threshold, even if you will have been married to her for thirty years?" I asked him.

"I sure will," he replied. "That is, if I can still lift her."

We said little about our future plans to anyone except the children. Another year passed. Correspondence flowed back and forth. There was no question of the approval of our own United Presbyterian Commission. Being a part of the National Council of the Churches of Christ, our representatives on the Christian Medical Council had been in on the early planning. Dr. Forman, our close friend of many years, reminded Fred of his unique qualifications for the position—his long experience in two of the largest mission fields, and his year with Doug Forman during a furlough. That he would be helping national doctors from many countries to do further graduate work in America was a facet of the complex job which appealed strongly to Fred, since his strongest call had always been to train nationals to carry on medical work in their own countries.

But after spending all the years of our life together in the overseas work of the Church, it was not easy to make the decision to leave it. We had planned to live and die here. And though Fred would still be doing mission work, we would not be called missionaries. We were rather proud of being called by that name. And we had to face squarely any feeling of guilt we might have in going home to comfortable America to live. Actually, Fred never had any such feeling. It was I who felt that I should explain it all to our colleagues. Fred said very simply, "God calls us to work for Him any place—as a garage mechanic, as a housewife, as a missionary."

Gradually it became clear to us that the new plan was God's call to us. We faced our own rationalizations and desires, knowing how easy it was to think that what we wanted to do was God's will. Still, under the given circumstances, this was the very best we knew how to do. The final decision was made.

From then on, everything we saw and did took on a different meaning. India had become home to us. Now instead of *living* in India, we were looking at all we experienced as if seeing it for the last time.

And there occurred one of those fortuitous happenings which seemed to complete the circle of the decision we had made. In a *Presbyterian Life* article, we read the story of the new recruit who would be the United Presbyterian replacement on the staff at Ludhiana. Dr. Donald Wysham, his wife, Dorothy, and their two small sons, would be arriving the summer after we were to leave. It was the sentence in the last paragraph of the article about the Wyshams which amazed us:

"Don can't be certain what tipped the scales in favor of a missionary career. Perhaps it was the twenty-four hours at Dr. Scovel's Center in Canton, an experience which greatly impressed the young doctor-to-be."

What I did not like at all about the new plan, was that Fred was to leave on Christmas Day to see more of the medical mission work of our own and other denominations. From now on, he would be helping with the overseas medical program of over one

hundred Protestant denominations. He would be gone until February. The East Asia Christian Medical Conference was meeting in Hong Kong. Here he would meet the doctors who were the national Christian leaders in their profession. He would then go on to Taiwan, Korea, Japan, the Philippines, Thailand, and Burma.

Our last Christmas in India was one of the strangest Christmases I have ever spent, shadowed as it was with Fred's impending departure that night. Too, we had to find a hippopotamus. Every time we asked Judy and Vicki what they wanted for Christmas that year, they replied in the words of a current popular song, "I want a hippopotamus for Christmas, and nothing but a hippo will do." Fred and I decided to give them one.

One of the ways which Mildred Hoffmeister devised for teaching arithmetic to the children of Ewing Christian School was to have them build animals to scale. She had on hand a life-sized

baby elephant, made of papier-mâché over a wooden frame. The school let us borrow it for the occasion.

In the black of night on Christmas Eve, amid many chuckles from Chandru and the servants he'd corralled to help him, the huge animal was carried through the compound on the shoulders of the men, and wedged into a dressing room at one end of our house. The elephant's hippopotamus-looking hind end completely filled the double doors at the entrance to the room from Fred's study. We arranged a maze of red and green yarn leading from the Christmas tree, through the house to the animal's tail, where we hung an envelope for each girl. Their gift was enough money to buy a sari each, and a few keepsakes from India to take home with them.

"What will you two do next?" asked Vicki, as we put a small ball of yarn in each of their hands and told them to start winding. Their faces when the yarn trail ended at the "hippo" were worth all the effort.

That afternoon Fred led the chapel service. It was a tradition of the college to invite for this service the leaders of the Christian community throughout the city.

Fred's words were always simply expressed, an outgrowth of his own spiritual seeking, and pertinent to the daily task. He asked us to consider that God had come to us as a Baby to show that He was willing to go through the long process of growing into manhood so that He could completely identify with us. We might, perhaps, consider the long years of His childhood to have been so much wasted time. The very nature of our work in mission called for a certain amount of efficiency. But God cared enough for us, not only to die for us, but to live with us!

The smiles on the faces across the chapel became one with his smile. The sight of him there in the pulpit made me know again that I could never deserve him.

After a supper with Myrtle and Raymond Cray, we came home long enough for Fred to pick up his bags and say a brief goodbye to each of the three of us. Then he was off for Hong Kong, and the big house was suddenly very big and very empty.

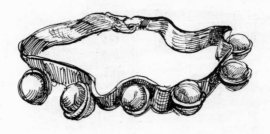

chapter seventeen

When Fred returned from the Orient in February of 1959, we had a glorious reunion. Judy, Vicki, and I met him at the airport in Delhi. I had one girl on either side of me, threatening to clap a hand over my mouth if I screamed when I saw him.

We "did the town" before our return to Ludhiana. The children had seen the poverty of India. Now we wanted them to see some of her opulence. As we got out of the taxi at the Ashoka Hotel, where we were to see the excellent murals of the life of Buddha, Vicki said, "Daddy, we aren't dressed for this at all."

"What do you mean?" asked her father. "We've all got clothes on, haven't we?"

"Yes, but what clothes!" she said, looking down at our six-year-old togs.

"Tell me, Mommy, how do you act in such a place?" Judy wanted to know.

By this time we were up a flight of stairs, and at the revolving doors.

"Just put your nose in the air, smile, and walk in like this," I said. I gave the door a push, caught my foot on the thick rug, and stumbled headlong into the main lobby, followed by two daughters and a husband, convulsed with laughter.

We returned from the plush life of Delhi to our own milieu at Ludhiana, and got the girls off for their last months at Woodstock School. Judy would graduate from high school that June; Vicki would be completing her freshman year.

Since we had to get our freight off early, and since I had a lot of writing to complete for the Indian Church, we moved out of our big house and took a room at Mildred Hoffmeister's. Mildred was on furlough, and our hostess was the principal of the school, Naomi Khazan Singh, who did not particularly want to stay alone in the house while Mildred was away.

Naomi's cousin was pastor of our church at the time. He used to drop in and see us in the evening to be sure that all was going well. Amos Boyd, our former pastor, and his family had gone to Saharanpur where Amos was teaching in the North India Union Theological Seminary. Fred and I had not wanted him to go. Amos felt it was God's leading; we were not so sure. We felt he was needed in Ludhiana. It was only when we heard of an incident at the Saharanpur church, that we were willing to agree that Amos had been right.

The church had badly needed renovating. Amos took his class of young seminarians into the church to ask them what they would do about it. Various methods of raising money were suggested.

Then their teacher took off his coat, opened a can of paint, and started to work. The young pastors-to-be were so stunned at seeing their professor stoop to such menial labor that for some time they just stood there watching him. At last one of them picked up a brush. Soon they were all having such a good time that young men of the congregation came in from the street to join the work crew. In no time at all, the church was completely renovated.

Perhaps we had been selfish in wanting our good friends, the

Boyds, to remain in Ludhiana. If they had, we might never have learned to know Padri Khazan Singh Stephens and his cousin, Naomi.

Naomi was a gentle woman with a beautiful serene face. She told us many stories of her father, who had also been a pastor. She remembered how he had bought baskets of mangoes each day during the mango season, and left them on the veranda so that his children could eat them all day if they wished. Naomi must have inherited her love for children from him. It was certain that she loved every one of the seven hundred and fifty little Sikhs, Hindus, and Christians in Ewing Christian School—as Mildred did.

"What do you think I was faced with this morning?" Naomi said at the table one noon.

"What?" we both asked at once, eager for one of her stories.

"One little rascal of ours has been giving us trouble for so long, that we reluctantly decided we'd have to give him a certificate of leaving," she began. "I told him yesterday to come into the office for it today. I dreaded it. We almost never do this, but we couldn't do a thing with this child, and he was disturbing classes so that the other children were being held up.

"Do you know what that child said when he came in this morning? He is only in fourth grade. He said, 'Miss Khazan Singh, don't give me that certificate. No other school will be any good for me. If you throw me out, I'll go to the bad. If you want to save a soul, keep me.' I leave you to guess what I did."

There was no doubt in our minds but that there still remained one little mischief-maker in Ewing Christian School.

Another time she told us of the Hindu child who came back to school after the Christmas holidays. "Your Christ came to our house," he told Naomi. "He wore old tattered clothes and was begging for food. I told my mother to bring him in and feed him because it was Christ, and she did."

Fred and I, without saying anything to each other aloud, began a series of this-will-be-the-last-time-we-evers. "It doesn't help to always be talking about it," Fred said.

There was a trip to the new capital of the Punjab to see Corbusier's modern buildings at Chandigarh. There was a trip to Amritsar to see the ancient Golden Temple of the Sikhs. There were calls on our friends, and farewell parties given by those with whom we had worked.

One such party was at the government School for Health Workers, with which our college was affiliated. Miss Sen, the vivacious person who ran it, was a Christian. She herself cooked the delicious food for the fifty of us. The number included her eighteen students, who helped in the preparation of the food and with the serving. Later we sat around the living room in small groups, talking.

"We shall miss you," said Miss Sen. "But God will take care of you. He always does. It has long been my personal experience—from the time I was a very young girl at school. Did I ever tell you about the time I lost my tithe money? No? It happened when I was in boarding school."

Because it was tithe money and belonged to God, she had washed the coins clean, then wrapped them in a white handkerchief and put them in a special place in her bureau drawer. When she went to get money for some good cause, she discovered that the little bundle had been stolen.

"I felt so bad about it," said Miss Sen, feeling again her childhood anguish. "I prayed that I might find them."

In the middle of the night, God told her to go to a certain upperclassman and ask her for the matron's keys. The three hundred trunks belonging to the students were kept in a large storeroom.

"When I went up to the girl's bed, awakened her, and asked for the keys, she simply reached under her pillow and gave them to me with no question," said Miss Sen. "Without any previous knowledge, I went straight to the trunk to which God directed me, chose the correct key, unlocked it, and there was my money! And the trunk belonged to a girl whom I would have least suspected.

"In the morning I told the matron I had taken her keys and why. But I did not give her the name of the thief.

"So God will watch over you. He will give you the keys to open the trunks he wishes you to open. Who knows? He may bring you back to us."

Miss Sen's psychical experience did not strike us as strange, nor as something she had imagined but which had never really happened. By now, we accepted such stories from our Indian friends as very real experiences. I had one such experience myself.

Before Tom left for school in America, he and his two closest pals, Bill McKelvey and Bren Burgoyne, attempted one of their Himalayan climbs—this one from Dharamsala, up into the snows,

fifteen thousand feet above sea level. One afternoon while he was away, I found myself sitting straight up in bed during a siesta, praying, "God, don't let him go after that camera." I could see Tom falling. I was covered with perspiration and prayed with every ounce of strength I had.

He came home a day early, arriving at night after I had gone to bed. The pedicab coming into the yard awakened me; then I heard Fred's voice, "You'd better wash the blood off that jacket before your mother sees you."

By this time, I was down the stairs and into the front hall. Tom turned pale when I said, "Tom, you didn't go after that camera when you dropped it, did you?"

He had. Knowing that he could never reach the top before dark if he went to search for it, and knowing that one of the boys was having trouble with his crampons, Tom took his off to give to his friend Bill. Using Tom's crampons, Bill might make the summit. As Tom went to look for his camera, he slipped and fell fifty feet, landing against the only rock which could have held him back from a three-thousand-foot fall.

Now I was to hear of another mystical experience—this time from a man we had not met before.

chapter eighteen

I was sitting in church at our last congregational meeting. Fred was up front with one of the other elders, Colvin Dayall; the two were counting the ballots for the election of officers. We were greatly relieved that this time there had been very little bickering between rival factions in the church, and no loud recriminations.

As I looked around the church, I thought of how much and how little had been accomplished in the one hundred and twenty-two years of its existence on this spot. If only John Lowrie had been allowed to carry out his original plan when he came here at the invitation of a Sikh leader in 1837! He never intended to found a mission; he wanted to found an indigenous Christian Church. It took us until November 21, 1956, to catch up with his thinking.

Fred and I would always be grateful that we had been present in this church on that historic moment when the mission ceased to exist, and the mission gavel was handed over to the Indian Church.

Our dear Herbert Strickler had presented the gavel to the Synod Moderator, the Rev. S. N. Talib-ud-Din. As Herbert Strickler rose to his feet, smiling, we thought of his many years of service to the Church in the Punjab. Not a person present but remembered his tragedy, and rejoiced that he had just been married to a lovely woman, a friend of many years.

"This gavel is just an ordinary thing made of wood," he had said. "It has even been broken a bit, perhaps by some one of us who lost his temper for a moment. But it is a mark of authority given as a symbol of our integration, our unity, our togetherness. May this convey with it not only the authority and responsibility of the past years, but also the joys and the blessings."

Fiery Padri Augustine Ralla Ram, in his speech on the history of the church, said, "If we of the Indian Church are going into this only to get more money and property, shame on us. There is so much more to be done. What are we planning to do about it?"

In any church, anywhere in the world, there was still so very much to be done! . . .

Fred and Colvin Dayall were still counting votes. Tension had drained out of the meeting. People were stretching their legs and walking around the church to visit with neighbors. I caught the face of an elderly gentleman I hadn't seen before. He was with the Superintendent of the Sunday School, a young member of our hospital staff, Mr. Macune. (McEwen, originally? I still couldn't get used to a Scot's name on an Indian or to an American name like Boyd. Many of the early Indian Christians were ostracized from their families and took the name of a beloved pastor or teacher.)

Mr. Macune brought the tall, scholarly gentleman over to meet me.

"This is Mr. Shadi Ram," he said. "He is a new convert to Christianity."

"Yes, but not through any man," said Mr. Shadi Ram. "My conversion came directly from God."

"What do you mean?" I asked.

"Tell her the whole story," said Mr. Macune.

Between Mr. Shadi Ram's telling it, and Mr. Macune's filling in the details, I learned what had happened.

He had been a Hindu pundit (a Brahmin versed in science, laws, and religion), greatly respected by the Hindu community which he served. But he himself was not satisfied that he had found the truth. He made a pilgrimage to the source of the Ganges, and worshiped there, seeking a peace he could not find. Upon his return, he made a study of the Sikh religion, but what he found in their holy book, the Granth, also failed to satisfy his longing.

One day during his meditation, he saw a face so filled with peace and beauty that he longed to know who it could be.

"After that vision, I remained in a trance for several days," said Mr. Shadi Ram. "Do you remember what happened to Paul after he had seen the Christ on the road to Damascus? It was like that with me. But I did not know it was the Christ I had seen, and of course, I had not heard of Paul.

"Months later, I heard a voice saying to me, 'Go to the Christian Church.' I did not want to go. It was raining very hard; I doubted if I would find a pedicab; I did not know where the church was. Above all, I did not like the idea of going to the Christian Church. But the voice persisted. So I said, 'If I am to go to the Christian Church, the rain will have to stop.' Immediately the downpour ceased. I was frightened."

He hurried out to the street and found at once a pedicab driver who knew where the church was.

"It was Sunday morning," Mr. Macune took up the story. "I was just going into the church for Sunday School. Shadi Ram asked me if he could talk to me. I hated to tell him that we would have to postpone our talk until the next day during my lunch hour, but what could I do? There were the six hundred children inside waiting for me.

"Then he asked me for something to read. 'Sir, you are a learned scholar,' I said. 'I cannot give you just anything to read. I have here only a little children's story I was just now going to use.' 'Give me anything; I must have something to read,' he said. So I gave him the little story and went inside, promising to meet him the next day at noon. From then on we have studied the Bible together all these months."

Mr. Shadi Ram had taken the little leaflet in Mr. Macune's hand, and there under the shade of the old, old tree, he opened to the frontispiece. It was the face of Christ as a Western artist had drawn Him.

"The very face I had seen in my vision," Mr. Shadi Ram told me. "Over the months, I would often become very discouraged as I waited for Mr. Macune to tell me I was at last ready for baptism. But in my disappointment, Christ would speak to me in the words of the Bible, 'You have not chosen me, but I have chosen you.' "

The new officers were about to be announced, and the two men returned to their seats. Wrapped in what I had just heard, I paid little attention to the outcome of the elections, except for being impressed that a woman had been elected as elder, while my little church in America had decided against having any women in that office.

"It speaks well for Indian women," I thought. "They have come a long way since the days of *purdah*." I went back to pondering the story of Mr. Shadi Ram.

If God could do what he did for Shadi Ram, why did he bother with us missionaries at all? At best we were a blundering, blithering lot, unable to speak the idiom of language after years of study; plowing with heavy boots through ancient culture and traditions. Why did God hamper himself with us when he could speak directly to men?

Then I thought of all it had taken to give Mr. Shadi Ram the peace he had been seeking. There *had been* a church for him to find. There *had been* a pedicab driver who knew the way. There *had been* a devoted, loyal man on the steps of that church in the course of performing his regular service to God. There was all that it took to build that church—in tithe money, in the giving by churches and individuals over the years in my own country. There were the men and women who had been the inspiration to those who had come as missionaries. There were the schools and the seminaries and the preaching and the disciplined writing which had gone into books on Bible study. And there was the artist who, true to his own inspiration, had painted a face recognizable as Christ to a Hindu half a world away.

If Fred and I had helped to form even the smallest link in that chain, it was a privilege of which we were not in the least worthy.

chapter nineteen

It was not until we had to pull our roots out of Indian soil that I realized how very deep they had grown and how painful would be the tug of their uprooting.

"Our teachers want to give you a farewell party," Naomi said one day during our last weeks with her. "What do you want most of all? *Please* tell me."

"Most of all I want to hear Kundan's *bhajan* singers once more," I told her.

Kundan was the cook. We had had to say goodbye to Chandru's family when we left our house. Chandru had gone back to his home in the hills before beginning his work for another family, and Balu went to work at the hospital. Kundan had cooked the first meal we had eaten in Ludhiana—breakfast that first morning with Mildred. Kundan was also a musician. He and the group of singers with whom he was associated often played in church, and Fred and I both loved this spontaneous, indigenous expression of praise to God. For these *bhajans*—hymns of praise—were written by Punjabis, and all Punjabis are poets.

After a delicious dinner, Kundan called in his singers and the instrument players with their drums, violin, and harmonium. They all sat down on the floor of the living room and began to sing in their usual lilting, syncopated rhythm. The main singer gave the first line of a couplet, the chorus repeated it. Then the soloist completed the couplet with a flourish, and the whole group triumphantly joined in a refrain. Some of the songs that night were composed on the spot, since they were messages of farewell to us. The light caught the earnest faces of the men as their bodies swayed to the rhythm of the song, a picture we would cherish.

There were the final photographs with our own medical students and one with *all* the students of Naomi's school (plus not only the elephant we had borrowed, but a life-sized giraffe which the children had made.)

There was the last call on old Miss Wylie, the Indian woman who lived alone in a large house across the street from the college. She was reputed to have forty thousand dollars hidden under her floors. We doubted it. What I would remember most were her stories of the first Christians in Ludhiana, which she told while the field mice ran across her threshold, and the sparrows pecked crumbs from the table where we were having our tea.

Perhaps two of the most difficult farewells to get through were the large party on the church lawn when each member of the congregation came forward to bid us goodbye, and our last tea with Dr. Eileen Snow. She dropped a soft white Kashmir shawl into my lap. It would always remind me of her; the borders were embroidered with all the midsummer flowers of an English garden.

A fabulous vegetarian dinner was prepared by my dear Hindu friend, Mrs. Sher Singh. Dr. Sher Singh was a radiologist at the

hospital. Their son, Dr. Chuttani, was Fred's closest associate in the medical department, and more of a son than an associate. He introduced us to many of the classical poets of India.

> *Ah, Qalib,*
> *Love is that fire*
> *Which cannot be kindled by lighting it,*
> *Nor can it ever be extinguished*
> *By extinguishing it,*

Dr. Chuttani would quote, and I would run for my notebook and pen.

It was at their home that we met the well-known woman poet, Baljit Tulsi Das. On two occasions she read to us her moving devotional poems in Punjabi.

On the night of our dinner with the Sher Singhs, we met the Sahni family, who were friends of the Sher Singhs. They told us that the male members of their family had, as a gift from God, the ability to cure guinea worm. It was done by making a few little marks, they did not say where. The secret was guarded jealously by the family, and passed down from generation to generation, but never to the female members of the family. They were not allowed to take money for it or to go out of their house to do it, but if anyone came to their door, they could cure him. Even their little four-year-old son had the ability to do this.

The last tea party was that given by the Jain Community at the instigation of Mr. Mul Raj, whom we had first met through the Garsts. His invitation was signed, as were all his notes to us, "Mul Raj, Jain." I wondered if I would ever dare to sign mine, "Myra Scovel, Christian." But this was one of the customs of the Jains. They were a break-off from Hinduism, a people who carried their reverence for life to what seemed to us extremes. We often met their white-dressed priests on the road, carrying a broom to sweep the way before them lest they step on any living thing. They also wore masks over the nose and mouth, lest they breathe in or swallow an insect.

Perhaps it was their great respect for life which gave Mul Raj, Jain, his interest in our hospital. He encouraged his friends in the community to build a rest home on the compound of the new hospital, so that relatives of patients would have a place to stay.

There was one painful ordeal for Fred to endure at that tea, the reading of a lengthy eulogy of what he had meant to the sick of Ludhiana and "indeed to the people of the state." I thoroughly enjoyed the experience, especially the final paragraphs which read:

> To you every patient, rich or poor, has been alike. The expert medical treatment, you gave to rich and poor, but you gave a little more love and affection to the poor sick. They shall always remember you with gratitude. Nothing has been below dignity to you. The sight of you carrying a trolley of instruments and other apparatus from one patient to another, shall keep flashing before our eyes, the very good example. In short, you have been the real disciple of the greatest Healer, The Lord Jesus Christ.

Now even the in-between period was over—that time when home no longer belongs to you, the time between the severing of the spirit from a place, and the final severing of the body. We were to leave for Landour before dawn next morning. We would spend a week with Judy and Vicki helping them with their packing, enjoying Judy's high school graduation, perhaps easing a little the terrible wrench of leaving friends with whom they had lived for six important years of their lives.

We would travel through Europe, and across the Atlantic. Then would come the reunion with our other children. Right now, I did not dare let myself think about it for fear it might not happen.

At four-thirty that summer morning, we walked out of the compound for the last time, in a crashing, booming thunderstorm.